The world of full-timing—living aboard a recreational vehicle—is an adventurous and affordable lifestyle. This book discusses the economic and social aspects of the lifestyle that now attracts thousands of retirees.

AN ALTERNATIVE LIVESTYLE

LIVING AND TRAVELING FULL-TIME
IN A RECREATIONAL VEHICLE

AN

ALTERNATIVE

LIFESTYLE

LIVING AND TRAVELING FULL-TIME
IN A RECREATIONAL VEHICLE

BY

RON & BARB HOFMEISTER

R & B PUBLICATIONS

First Edition May, 1992
Revised Edition August, 1993
Second Printing January, 1994
Third Printing August, 1994
Fourth Printing January 1995

ISBN 0-9637319-0-4
Library of Congress Card Number 94-185-084

Printed in the United States at Morgan Printing, Austin, Texas
Cover and design— Dale Wilkins Art, Austin, Texas

This book is dedicated to

Our families—they have learned, along with us, how the joys of full-timing enrich our relationships.

Our friends along the way—you welcomed us, taught us and befriended us. We treasure you, our new friends.

Our friends we left behind—thanks for remembering us and keeping in touch. We haven't forgotten you.

CONTENTS

ACKNOWLEDGEMENTS

Our original book, on full-time living in a recreational vehicle, began taking shape in 1990. Since that time, and one revision later, we are indebted to some very special people. As we struggled with the mechanics of both books, Mark and Terry along with the competent staff at Morgan Printing, were there to give encouragement and cheerful help. Your patience and skills will always be appreciated.

Warren and his gang at The Hill Country Community Press in Fredricksburg, Texas, helped us meet deadlines with excellent quality photo work (half-tones) contributing to all the wonderful photographs in the book. Our thanks to you.

We owe a debt of gratitude to Edward Richmond, a reader from Pennsylvania, who kindly coached us on the mechanics of the English language. We appreciated his gentle and constructive critique.

Many thanks to Bette Salter who wandered into our life at a time when we were struggling with the final editing. This retired school teacher graciously accepted the job of editing the majority of the book while she and her husband, Clyde, were camped across from us in Spicewood, Texas.

And many more thanks to long time friend, Norma Neve, who went over the entire book again with her sharp eagle eye and listed each and every forgotten comma, typo, improper hyphenation, etc., so we could fix them before the third printing.

Finally, we want to acknowledge two good friends, without whom, this book might not have been completed. Without a doubt, it was the gentle prodding (nagging?) and encouragement of Nancy Joy and Judy Richards that kept us on track. Thanks to all of you. What a team.

PREFACE

This book is about an exciting, glamorous, fulfilling, and surprisingly affordable lifestyle that is particularly attractive to retired people. This way of life has become so popular that close to a million (mostly retirees) have adopted it. People enjoying this carefree lifestyle are called full-timers. They are people who live *full-time* in an RV (recreational vehicle) and *travel* in that vehicle.

"Full-time" and "travel" are the key words here. Many people live full-time in a travel trailer and the unit is seldom moved. Others (usually retirees) take their RVs south for the winter and many people take extended trips (sometimes months) in their RVs, but they always go back to a permanent home. These people are not full-timers as we use the term in this book.

The full-timers that we are writing about *do not* have a home other than the RV that they live in, and they can be found traveling the United States as well as Mexico and Canada. Full-timers may have a few personal things in a small storage locker or at a relative's home, but there is no traditional home. The RV *is* home. The concept of not having a permanently based home is important because of the economic implications which we will discuss in this book.

We started our full-timing life on March 30, 1989. Since that time, we have traveled through forty-one states, living exclusively in our motorhome, and are more enthusiastic than ever about our chosen lifestyle. Our original plans called for settling down after two or three years, but now we can't imagine doing that.

There are several books and many articles on full-timing, and for the most part they are interesting and motivational. Unlike the others, this book will deal, in depth, with the social and economic aspects of the lifestyle. We will discuss the good as well as the bad days. At the end of each chapter we will add an article from our diary, letters, or *Movin' On* (our newsletter). These articles will give a personal glimpse into full-timing.

Since one of the authors is a retired finance director, we will look closely at the financial aspect of full-timing. Although full-timing can be an economical lifestyle, this book is not about living frugally. We don't suggest parking in shopping center parking lots and roadside rest areas overnight to save money. People on limited retirement incomes may successfully full-time using a variety of money saving strategies; however, our approach will emphasize full-timing as a lifestyle rather than an economic necessity.

This is not a book about repairs either. Most "how to" full-time books go into much detail on the inner workings of the RV. Instead, we have included a list of reference publications that will aid those seeking cost-cutting ideas. These publications provide information on free campsites as well as do-it-yourself repair methods.

A laptop computer has enabled us to accumulate and analyze every expenditure made since March 30, 1989. All expenditures were recorded. Campground fees, gasoline costs, maintenance costs and all other expenses were tabulated and averaged—even the quarters spent in the laundromat.

For many, the economics of full-timing will take a back seat to the social aspects of this nomadic lifestyle. At first glance there are enough problems to scare off even the most adventurous. Leaving family and friends, receiving mail, handling financial affairs, dealing with mechanical breakdowns, and organizing travel schedules typify the problems that people

Preface

ask us about. We will discuss them all candidly with you. Most logistical problems, if not all, can be planned for. In the following chapters we will discuss them in detail. Unexpected problems—we call adventures.

The first printing of this book has sold out and the response has been gratifying. When planning a second printing, we looked at that chapter of our book dealing with change. We found that, in just a year, our full-timing adventure has been filled with changes. We hope that it is always that way. Rather than a reprinting, we have incorporated some of these changes in a second edition of *An Alternative Lifestyle*. In this second edition you will note that we have changed motorhomes and have reinforced our personal preference for motorhomes as a full-timing vehicle. Since the first edition, Barb has changed her ideas on what a well supplied kitchen should have especially since moving to a larger motor home. She has added more newsletter articles in order to share with you the joy of some of these changes.

Our first book failed to recognize that there are many single people enjoying our lifestyle. They have helped us put together some information on that aspect of full-timing. In this edition we discuss briefly (because you asked) pets and security on the road. We have enjoyed corresponding with many of you and have benefited from your suggestions. We have found that full-timers are flexible and ready for new adventure. The one thing that hasn't changed is our enthusiasm for the full-timing lifestyle.

We do not see our lives as complicated and full of problems, in fact, we are similar to a lot of other retirees. We visit family, do laundry, go for drives in the country, grocery shop, play cards with friends, dine out, golf, read, attend potlucks, go to church, clean house, watch movies, and walk the malls. However, our house is small, and we have no yard to maintain. For us, there's much more time to play.

The big difference between us and other retirees is that we move—sometimes once a week—sometimes once a month. We move whenever we feel like it. And always around the corner there is a new place to see and new people to meet. We could spend a lifetime (and probably will) seeing this beautiful land and not see it all. In those states we have already visited, there are many towns, villages, parks, mountains, seashores and historical sites that we missed the first time through. There are many places we would like to revisit and stay longer. So much to see and experience, so little time to do it. Let's get going then. Explore with us the ins and outs of full-timing; after which, you may decide to join us.

♥   ♥

1

FULL-TIMING

An Overview

The concept of full-timing is fairly simple. Today's modern motorhomes, travel trailers, and fifth-wheels provide comfortable accommodations even though they are a good deal smaller than the average home. Our first motorhome was not a large one, and although our new one is bigger, it is not as big as a small apartment. But we have the United States as a back yard. Since we are generally in warm weather, much of our time is spent outdoors. Even if it's raining, we can use the picnic table under our awning.

It's not necessary to leave conveniences behind. Today's RV is equipped with a refrigerator and freezer (operating on both

electric and propane), televisions (sometimes two), air conditioning, microwave oven, conventional oven, and many other
options, depending on the model and pocket book. Some have
a washer and dryer, and friends of ours even have a small
water softener in their motorhome. Another couple we know
has a dishwasher. Our favorite on-board possessions are a
laptop computer, a full size PC (personal computer) and
printer. The laptop computer works (with attachments) on
either alternating or direct current, depending on whether we
are plugged into a power source at a campground or in a
remote area using our house battery.

The goal then, of a full-timer, is a different lifestyle, not a
harder one. This comfortable lifestyle is possible when com-
bining a modern RV with the availability of thousands of public, private and membership campgrounds all over the United
States, Canada and Mexico. There are also many scenic spots
where camping is permitted even though it is not designated
as a campground where full-timers can call home for a while.

Full-timers can "live" in a country club type park complete
with luxurious full hook-up sites, heated pools, hot tubs,
sports courts, billiard rooms, ballrooms, and restaurants.
These parks often have a professional activities director, and
guests can keep very busy with everything from wood working
to square dancing. Other commercial campgrounds are comfortable with wide, beautifully landscaped sites, full hookups,
and a pool complex without all the scheduled activities. Most
have a nice lounge where folks can gather for cards and
games. Some have big screen TVs and weekend breakfasts or
once a week potlucks. The price ranges are as wide as the
amenities offered.

On the other end of the scale, the remoteness of a state or
national park campground has its own appeal. Instead of TV,
entertainment consists of watching the wildlife, beautiful
scenery and sunsets. Instead of the radio, music comes from
the birds and the wind rustling through the trees. And instead
of tennis, exercise is walking or hiking the trails. The hookups

range from full (rare), to water and electric (more common), to rustic (bare bones—wilderness type), and the prices are very reasonable.

The concept becomes more interesting when considering the economic aspects of full-timing. Campground fees take the place of rent, utilities, property tax, maintenance costs, and other fees associated with home ownership. We have budgeted $175 a month for campground fees and have not hesitated to treat ourselves to some luxury sites (in addition to membership parks) when we feel like it. After four years of full-timing, we find this figure excessive because public park fees, membership parks, and occasional free parking offset the cost of luxury parks. In the luxury parks, monthly rates are often within our budget. Many full-timers think that our $175 budget is extravagant because they boondock—either out of necessity or just plain fun.

Boondocking means camping free. It can be anywhere. Boondockers may camp in roadside rest areas, on beaches, shopping center parking lots, church parking lots, deserts, fair grounds and almost anywhere they can safely and legally park. Sometimes it's just for overnight in a rest area, or for many days in a scenic spot on the desert or on a beach. Often other boondockers are camped in the same area adding to the fun. The practice requires a self-contained RV (which most are), and ingenious methods of providing electricity and water to the RV for extended stays. Therefore, good water conservation methods and efficient waste disposal are a way of life with the long term boondocker. We will not be discussing in-depth methods of boondocking. If interested in learning about this facet of full-timing, we recommend reading *Survival of the Snowbirds,* by Joe and Kay Peterson, founders of the Escapees Club. To obtain a copy of this book write to *RoVers Publications, Route 5, Box 310, Livingston, Texas, 77351.* The cost is $8.95 plus $1 postage and handling.

Whatever the camping preference, it's available in this wonderful land of ours. Our personal preference is campgrounds with full facilities interspersed with stop offs at national parks. We have a goal to visit every national park in the continental United States, and we are well on our way. We use full service parks because, after all, we DO live in our RV year round. It's not like we are on a short camping trip, after which we will go home to all the conveniences. We like electricity and running water and don't mind having heated swimming pools, saunas, hot tubs and tennis courts either.

Although there are some young people, and a fair number of Baby Boomers full-timing, the nomadic lifestyle is particularly attractive to retirees for obvious reasons. Most retirees have left the job market and no longer have day-to-day family responsibilities. Full-timers have discovered that even with a modest income (in some cases only social security), they can enjoy a satisfying, travel filled retirement previously available only to the wealthy. This is possible because their full-time wanderings represent their total daily living expense. They are relieved of maintaining a house or apartment and the concerns associated with absentee ownership. The financial aspects of full-timing are discussed fully in Chapter 10. Financial considerations will be an important part of this book.

In 1988, the television program, *20/20* presented a segment dealing with full-timers, and estimated that there were approximately 200,000 of us in the United States. Dr. Roberta Null, at the University of Miami of Ohio, recently profiled the full-timer and found 90 percent are over the age of 50, have incomes between $15,000 and $30,000, and 90 percent are married. There are many social and economic considerations involving the decision to be a full-timer, and we will also discuss those.

The first question that arises deals with the type of recreational vehicle to be used. Many retirees already own an RV that they have been using for vacations or weekend camping trips. Some of these units may be suitable for full-timing if in good condition. The type of unit chosen will involve a lot of tradeoffs. If buying a new or used RV consider the following items as they affect full-timing plans: average planned length of stay, economic resources, driving skill, space needs, hobbies, geographic terrain to be traveled, local travel and sightseeing, and most important of all—personal preferences. The three major types of RVs that we will discuss are a travel trailer, fifth-wheel and motorhome.

What is the most popular choice among the three major RV categories? It's difficult to say, and to our knowledge there hasn't been a survey of full-timer's preference. Our unscientific observations in southern RV parks seem to split out evenly between the three types. These observations, however, may not represent full-timers, since many of the travel trailers belong to "snowbirds" who tend to stay at one park for the winter before returning to a permanent home. A travel trailer (because it doesn't move for three or four months) may best serve their needs. In addition, most are still maintaining a home in the north country, and the trailer represents less of an investment for the three or four months that it is used. The full-timers that we meet on the road are usually in a motorhome (towing a car) or a fifth-wheel. All of these units, and combinations of units, have tradeoffs which we will explore in Chapter 3.

How about spending 24 hours a day with a mate? You will undoubtedly miss the family. But will that be a problem? How do full-timers keep in touch with the family? These are good questions that need to be explored and Chapter 8 will do that. Another question involves banking and handling daily financial needs, and this book deals with that.

Many have shared our experience and found that other full-timers are truly neighbors. They love to help and give advice. Many times we have changed our itinerary because someone said, "You simply can't miss this or that." And guess what—they were right. We would have missed such places as Carlsbad Caverns and White Sands New Mexico. We learned about screen door latches and solar panels from a lovely campground host couple in the Smoky Mountains National

Park. Learn about campground hosting in Chapter 6. On North Padre Island, Texas, we learned about the many types of generators available and which ones are quieter. And in Mission, Texas, we had all kinds of advice on washing our motorhome and patching a leaky waste water tank. We are never alone.

Once the decision is made to full-time, is it irreversible? Absolutely not! Most full-timers know that someday because of health or other good reasons, they may pull off the road. This does not present a problem, and if that time ever comes (we hope it doesn't) it's surprising how easy the transition can be made. We feel that it need not be a financial problem because we have actually saved money.

So far, we have given you an overview as to what full-timing is, who does it, why they do it, what equipment they use, and where they stay. To give an example of what our life is like, we would like to describe a few weeks from our first year on the road. The scene is a very neat campground in San Antonio, Texas. It has wide campsites and full hookups for $10.70 a night on a weekly basis. During the day we did the laundry at the campground laundromat and did some writing for this book. In the late afternoon we went down to the famous river walk where the whole city was celebrating the final day of Carnival Del Rio (a take-off on Mardi Gras). Dinner was a delightful experience at an outdoor cafe along the river. The next day we visited the Alamo and four historic missions that comprise the San Antonio Missions National Historic Park.

The following week found us in Corpus Christi where we spent a week on North Padre Island ($4 a night and right on the gulf). Next stop was Mission, Texas, where we stayed for three weeks in order to get some minor maintenance done and to relax with golf, tennis, and walking. The country club type RV resort we stayed at was typical of many that are available throughout the country. Many of the membership campgrounds have similar facilities. What they all have in common, however, are the people staying there. They have time for conversation and fun. Like so many others where we have stayed, we enjoyed the card games in the evening and meeting people at the get-togethers. After three relaxing weeks and many new friends, it was on to Big Bend National Park, Texas, for hiking, breath taking scenery, ranger programs, more new friends and some beautiful rustic camping. And on and on and on.... Full-timing makes this type of life possible, because for most of us, it would not be affordable if we had to maintain a home or pay for motels and other travel expenses.

But, it's not for everyone. The following chapters will explore this lifestyle. You may decide to join us. If you do, we can be anywhere. We may be under a pine tree in a national park, or biking through gorgeous autumn leaves in Vermont, or hiking a trail in a national park, or maybe just enjoying a campfire in a beautiful state park in northern Michigan. We may also be pool side enjoying the luxuries of a membership park, visiting your church on a Sunday, or shopping at your grocery store. Wherever we are, we will be looking for you. Our redwood sign is on the front of the motorhome—our home. We have a guest book that we would love for you to sign and the coffee pot is always on.

♥   ♥

From Our 1989 Christmas letter

...We thought that you'd like to know what we've been up to in the eight months since we took to the vagabond life. **It has been everything that we wanted it to be.** When we left Haslett on March 30, it was cold and rainy, and it remained that way for the first three weeks of our new life. Even though the weather kept us confined to our "little" house a lot, we did not get claustrophobia. We even continued to like each other and figured we had it made from then on. We have plenty of room and eventually purchased a few new things like our Toshiba laptop computer and a Panasonic printer.

We took a month to get to Florida, stayed there for three weeks and took 10 days to get back to Michigan (that was too fast for us too). We were having such fun that we really didn't want to come back and get ready to go on our scheduled trip to England. On June 13, we put our "house" in storage and drove to Detroit Metro Airport. At the airport, we took the bikes off the roof of the car, grabbed our panniers (saddle bags), and wheeled our bikes into the airport. About two hours later, we were on our way to London. It was a strange feeling—no luggage and everything we needed for six weeks was in those panniers....

Before leaving Michigan again, we bought 15-½ acres of heavily wooded (hard wood) property in Leelanau County. It is only six miles south of Leland and approximately two miles from Lake Michigan (as the crow flies). Someday, if we ever get tired of this life, we can build a log cabin and settle down. We didn't leave Michigan until the end of August and since then have spent a lot of time in upstate New York, Vermont, New Jersey, Pennsylvania, W. Virginia, Virginia, North and South Carolina and now are in Florida. It has been fun becoming Civil War buffs—touring the major battle fields as we came across them.

We have met wonderful people along the way. Some will

become life time friendships. It is a little difficult continually adjusting to new towns and their grocery stores; but, all in all it has been a joy. I am typing this letter while sitting under a cover of big oak and palm trees in the Ocala National Forest Campground. Enchanting noises made by the tropical birds provide the sounds of a jungle. Ron is preparing to start our campfire and soon will be ready to grill some chicken. Such is our life. And we love it except for one thing. We miss all our friends and family back in Michigan; but on the other hand we have been able to re-acquaint ourselves with family and old friends who live far away.

♥ ⌂ ♥

2

IS THIS FOR US?

Often in our travels, we have heard these comments, "I would love to do what you are doing, but my wife (husband) is too attached to our home. He (she) would never leave the children (grandchildren)." "I couldn't bear to part with our possessions." "I have to have a home to come back to." These are real concerns, but let's explore them from a different perspective as they relate to the full-timing lifestyle. There is no one way to full-time, and it's interesting to see how others have tailored their equipment and schedules to meet their own particular needs.

It's true that, for some people, the uncertainty and simplicity of a nomadic life detracts from the adventurous prospect of travel and seeing new sights. Heirlooms, hobbies, lawns, gardens, beautiful homes, cherished possessions, friends and family would be too much to leave behind when contemplating full-timing. That is understandable.

In our situation, although we stored some favorite possessions (photo albums, pictures, organ, etc.) in a storage locker, there were some material things that we missed at first. We miss gardening, Saturday night pinochle with several close friends and our favorite Chinese restaurant. That is, we miss these things until we start to climb Guadalupe Mountain in West Texas or drive to the top of White Face Mountain at Lake Placid or enjoy a Mexican dinner in a small bar in the remote area of Desert Center, California. You get the idea. The list of things we miss is very small compared to what we would miss if this lifestyle were to end. When we think of our daily adventures, experiences, and new friendships, it would be difficult to imagine going back to a conventional existence.

Imagine visiting twenty-two national parks, dozens of historical parks and national monuments, Lake Placid, Vermont in the Fall, the Everglades, Key West, the French Quarter in New Orleans, famous restaurants, a Cajun swamp, a Texas ranch, a Texas observatory, ancient cliff dwellings in New Mexico, and Las Vegas in less than four years. Can you also imagine visiting several ghost towns, Rose Bowl and Tournament of Roses, Hollywood, Alcatraz Island, Golden Gate Park, Civil War battlefields, Amish country, Washington, D.C., a battleship in Norfolk, beautiful mountain ranges, deserts, glaciers, volcanos, giant redwoods, coastal seashores, historic houses, Mexican border towns and thousands of small towns and villages in that same four years? We can because we have done it, in addition to twelve months of volunteer work in national parks (three months at a time) and two and one-half months off (two different trips) to bicycle across England, Wales and Ireland. Do we miss playing pinochle on Saturday nights with our old friends? Sure we do. It's a tradeoff and it doesn't have to be forever.

Back to "things." Although it helps to think small, full-timers manage to include many of those items that they have always enjoyed. This is particularly true when it comes to sports equipment. Almost every full-timer carries bicycles and fishing gear, and it's not uncommon to see boats and/or canoes being carried on the roof of the tow vehicle. In addition, many carry golf clubs, bowling balls and tennis rackets. Leisure time possessions are not limited to sports equipment either. We have seen painting easels and supplies, computers, craft tools, sewing machines, and one full-timer even included his wood working tools. We recently saw a 30-foot motorhome towing a trailer with a helicopter on top. How about that for a pull toy?

The thought of missing friends, family, church and familiar surroundings is a concern and may cause many to be uncertain about full-timing. However, those contemplating full-timing are not the only ones who face this problem. Many retirees elect to relocate to a smaller house, apartment or condo for purposes of lower taxes, less upkeep, warmer climates, rural settings and other good reasons. In spite of the initial apprehension most of the changes turn out for the better.

We thought that Mom and Dad would surely be back within two years when they retired to Florida. That was 25 years ago. It was the best time of their lives with dozens of new friends and a new church they loved. The new friends had time to play because they were retired too. The community was geared to their needs and preferences. Family didn't seem to be a problem because now there was time for quality visits with no distractions. They were fortunate because there were many visits from family, especially in the winter. What offspring wouldn't want to leave a northern winter for a visit to the sunny South? Sure there were times when they missed the family, but you can miss family when you are only ten miles away.

It helps to remember that, similar to transplanted retirees, full-timers can have their families visit. We found that grandchildren love a camping experience, and it is easy to have them join us in the summer when school is out. Our two young granddaughters accompanied us to a Yogi Bear camp-

Mary, Grandpa & Erika at bedtime

ground for a couple of days one summer and they still talk about that trip and the fun around the campfire.

Another time, while volunteering at Yosemite National Park in California, granddaughter Liisa came to visit us for two weeks. At the age of twelve, and already experienced with flying alone, she flew to Fresno. Not only did she get to live in and explore the nation's most beautiful national park, she also worked there. Yes, worked! She joined us in portraying pioneers in the living history center. Our park ranger supervisor was delighted to have her dressed up and playing the part of Minnie, a young pioneer child. Like us, Liisa had to research her character and "live" the part when the center was open. Visitors couldn't get over how thoroughly she portrayed life in the late 1800s. It was a vacation she will never forget.

Like many retirees, chances are full-timers will be where it's warm in the winter time—a good place for family to visit. It can still be an inexpensive vacation for them if they are campers. We think of the magnificent southern resorts where we have stayed, or some of the beautiful parks, such as the Ocala National Forest campground in Florida. It would be so much fun to share this with family. We know most of our visitors would enjoy the pool, hot tub, shuffleboard and other games that many resort parks offer. Every location has it's special attractions. For example, a visit to a southwestern state could include an afternoon of shopping and lunch across the border in Mexico. Everyone who has been to a national park knows about the wide range of activities that families can enjoy there. Son Robert, who has visited us at several different campgrounds in California and Florida as well as Traverse City, Michigan, and Snoqualmie, Washington, said, "Gee, Mom, it's neat that you are *home* wherever I go."

Unlike other retirees, we move around, and our family can enjoy the new locations and explore right along with us. Visits need not be limited to family. When we were volunteering at Hot Springs National Park, it was fun to share experiences with longtime friends, Brenda and Judith who came to visit the beautiful area. Because we were knowledgeable about the park, we could be their personal guides and add to their visit. Many have told us that they want to visit at our next volunteer assignment.

When it's your turn to visit, it's easy to visit family members at their homes. We have found, that since we are mobile, visits to our children, wherever they might be, can be longer and less expensive. And isn't it better to sleep in your own bed while parked in son or daughter's back yard where the grandchildren can join you for breakfast in *your* kitchen? Ours do. Our grandchildren love to come out and wake up grandma and grandpa by jumping on the bed.

It's also economical to visit when considering that the RV is the only home; and rent, house payments and other expenses are not accumulating while away. Nor are there any campground fees. That allows extra money for special treats like taking the kids out for dinner. In lieu of driveway fees, baby sitting is always appreciated and a great way to enjoy the grandchildren.

We can't leave the subject of family visits without emphasizing the concept of quality visits. Several years ago we missed a family reunion. It included aunts, uncles, sisters and brother along with their children. We happened to be cycling across England at the time (but that's the subject of another book). Later, in our full-timing travels we did get to visit *all* of the aunts and uncles, spending a few days with each one as we traveled across the country.

During one of our visits, Uncle Don said, "You know, at the reunion, I really didn't get to visit much with my brothers because there were too many of us, lots of commotion and not enough time. Besides, they were all busy with their own families." How sad, but true. With one-on-one visits there is time for long evening chats exchanging experiences and pictures, not to mention reminiscing of childhood times. We carried that one step further in Hornell, New York, where Barb was born. We enjoyed visiting childhood friends and hangouts (soda fountains, the old Woolworth dime store, etc.) and looked up old family residences and ancestral cemetery plots. To top it all off, we attended the Hornell High School homecoming game with three uncles and their families. Hornell won, but it wouldn't have mattered if they had lost because we were having fun with family and going back in time.

With a few differences, full-timers have much in common with the seniors that relocate when they retire. Although we meet many people daily and develop strong permanent friendships, they are not next door every day. Friends are scattered all over the United States.

For many, church activities are an important part of life. It's natural to think about missing your church, but full-timing is an opportunity to enrich spiritual life not only in church attendance but in daily devotions that we never seemed to have time for before. We have our devotions just before breakfast—what a neat way to start the day.

There are many churches of every denomination in America, but sometimes it takes a little effort to find out the times and location of services. We carry a church directory of our faith that lists starting times and addresses wherever we are; and we usually buy a local paper that provides similar information, including any church suppers in the area. Even with all these precautions, we get crossed up occasionally. We arrived to an empty church in upstate New York one Sunday morning, where they had switched services temporarily to Saturday night in order to accommodate their visiting minister during a pastoral vacancy. Now we scout out the church a day or two before Sunday and note travel time and time of service. In spite of some unexpected events, we love visiting a different church every Sunday and find that it contributes to our religious life. It gives us pleasure to know that many share our beliefs, and we find a special fellowship worshiping with others in our faith.

We have particularly enjoyed small country churches where we are often asked to introduce ourselves to the congregation. You can imagine the reaction when we say that our home is our motorhome, and it always leads to conversation and new friendships. In Ocean Springs, Mississippi, a couple we were talking to after church (Mary Ann and Jim), were very interested in what we were doing. That afternoon they joined us with their bikes at the national park, suggesting a bike ride into town for a personalized tour. They also talked us into staying an extra week to see the annual Mardi Gras parade.

We have listened to outstanding choirs, dynamic preachers and worshiped in beautiful friendly churches. Some of our worship experiences have been unusual. We will never forget the minister in Key West, Florida, who stopped in the middle of the liturgy to introduce his sister who had arrived. His

First Lutheran—Grand Marais, Michigan

sermon (probably written over breakfast) was just as folksy and informal with very little continuity. Sixteen hundred miles north at Grand Marais, Michigan, on Lake Superior, we felt close to the devout congregation of 20 souls being served by a visiting minister. He had traveled over a hundred miles one way to be at that remote location. Several weeks later, and much further south, at Davison, Michigan, we were informed that services were being held in a big tent behind the church. Sure enough, an overflow crowd was gathering under two large tents to usher in the fall season with a pig roast scheduled right after church. During church we could smell the pig as it was turning on the spit nearby. A young musical group provided outstanding professional music and song as we joined the joyous mood of the congregation. We consider our church attendance as part of our lifestyle. At least when we have a different minister or liturgy every Sunday, we are less likely to fall asleep. Worship becomes less rote and more meaningful.

It's true that people are often attached to possessions or a house, and for them a gradual transition to full-timing may work best. Everyone has different needs and giving up or limiting one's possessions may be too big a step at one time. For these people, it's best to enter the world of full-timing cautiously. Certain prized treasures or favorite items can be stored. Anything beyond a small rented storage area becomes expensive, but it may be worth the extra expense to store more—at least for a couple of years. Perhaps a son or daughter may have unused space that can provide a viable option.

Some full-timers may rent their house, not only to provide income, but to keep their options open. Those that do, often employ a professional management company to look after the house and collect the rent in order to avoid the problems of an absentee landlord. All of the above options provide a security blanket of sorts.

One of our favorite "things" is a plaque on the wall of our motorhome that says, "The best things in life aren't things." Most of the full-timers we have met do not appear to be hung-up on material things, but rather on **living**. It's a good thing too, because room is at a premium in any RV. If the RV is large with lots of storage, more can be carried. If not, think of all the money saved by not buying unneeded items. We do not, however, live like misers. We like to buy new things, but usually discipline ourselves to replace rather than accumulate. Earrings and computer software programs are small and can be stored easily. If visiting the west, it may be important to have a cowboy hat and a fancy belt buckle. We just buy different things and think small. Those who are into large beautiful homes with all the furnishings and conveniences may not be good full-timing candidates. We think that **You** are different or you wouldn't have picked up this book.

There are many different ways of approaching full-timing. For some, full-timing means *full-time camping*. Others have a large luxury type RV and stay exclusively in private campgrounds with full hookups. For those who elect to stay exclusively in public parks or boondock, full-timing can become a rustic existence. What does that mean? It might mean cooking outside over a camp stove when it's too hot to cook inside. If bathroom quarters are cramped in the RV, or if water is scarce, it will probably be a good idea to use the public shower facility—if there is one. In most national parks there are no showers. This means getting used to the world of sponge baths. When boondocking in the desert (not for everyone) even sponge baths can be a luxury. Lack of electricity should not be a concern, even in remote locations, because of the availability of solar panels, storage batteries and generators. However, water and waste disposal can be a problem. It's not unusual to have to refill water tanks and/or dump the waste water tanks after a week or two in a rustic area. It all adds up to a camping experience, and it becomes second nature to allow for, and think of, these little chores. That is—if one is a camper. It's no secret that experienced campers find the transition to this style of full-timing much easier. Some full-timers still remember tent camping with fond memories and they like rustic camping.

An everyday camping experience may not be your cup of tea. It doesn't have to be. If you are like us, a little of the rustic style is all right, but let's not get carried away. After all, full-timing is our everyday life—not just a two-week vacation. We want to be comfortable and enjoy all of the conveniences that make life pleasant. We have found that most full-timers do not opt for the heavy camping experiences that we have been discussing. They belong to one of several membership campgrounds and travel the United States going from one campground to another. There they experience a camaraderie with fellow members and enjoy the amenities of the private campground and all the luxuries that go with it. One is apt to find a lot of full-timers in membership parks. In Chapter 5, we discuss the advantages of belonging to a membership park. There are a lot of us who space visits to national and state parks in between the luxury and conveniences of a member-ship park. That way we have the best of both worlds.

How about rainy days? Some of the best days are rainy days. Rainy days are good days to visit a mall, go to a movie, read, listen to music or even take a nap—not unlike your cur-rent life. If in a public park, especially in the spring or fall, it's possible to have the whole park to yourself. After all, people on vacation or long weekends don't *have* to go camping. We like the experience of having the whole park to ourselves, but some people may find that to be lonesome. We remember visiting Brown County State Park in southern Indiana one spring. It had been raining for several days and no one was there. Suddenly the rain stopped and the park was alive with deer and other wild life. We really weren't alone after all.

Rainy days and empty parks lead us to the most important facet of full-timing. We will deal with it right up front. **You had better consider your spouse as your best friend.** It is extremely important that you enjoy each other's company and **enjoy doing things together.** There is no retreating into a workshop or sewing room, and the RV can be close quarters, especially in inclement weather. That doesn't mean that everything must be done together, and certainly it can be arranged to have time apart. One couple we know take their walks separately, and rather than shop and do laundry to-gether, they each do one job so they can be alone. It is especially helpful when one partner can escape for a day of shopping or visiting with friends. That is why it is so important to have transportation other than the RV itself.

In spite of these breaks, let's face it—spouses will be spending a lot of time together and will rely on each other for companionship. It is helpful to have common interests and hobbies such as reading, biking, hiking, golf, or just plain sightseeing. We met another couple who were worlds apart on how to spend their time. His idea of a great life was to simply sit in the campground talking to other campers with an occas-ional day of fishing thrown in. He opted for month-long stays in campgrounds and wasn't interested in venturing far from the original home. The other in this marriage hungered for sightseeing, wanted to go to national parks and visit historic sites. When last we heard, he was building her a house so he could take off to some campground.

Our game box includes over a dozen games. We would rather play games, with a bowl of popcorn next to us, than watch television. We also like to just talk. By now you can tell that we are friends—best friends. It's essential for this kind of lifestyle. What can be better than being on a perpetual vacation seeing the United States with your best friend?

Is this lifestyle for you? Only you and your spouse can answer that question. If what you have just read sounds like fun, you are part way there.

♥　♥

From Our 1990 Christmas Letter

Dear Friends,

We wish you a Joyous Holiday Season and the Happiest of New Years!!!

As we began to think about Christmas and the year coming to an end, we reflected on our past year and thought you would like to know where we went, what we did and if we still like our full-timing lifestyle.

Last New Year's Eve found us in Central Florida. We published our first newsletter in January and have printed one each month since then. From Florida, we spent most of our time slowly inching west until we ended up in California. Then we went back to Michigan for the Summer.

We were in Mississippi and Louisiana in January enjoying national seashore parks, warm hospitality, Mardi Gras and good food. A new grandson was born on January 29. Kristopher was born in England to son Jim and his wife Sue.

We enjoyed two fantastic months in Texas (February and March). What contrasts: the big city of Houston, the quieter and lovely Austin and San Antonio areas, the lively Rio Grande area full of retirees ready to party, the remoteness of Big Bend and Guadalupe Mountain National Parks. We danced, played lots of tennis and bridge, enjoyed family visits, climbed mountains—we just had lots of fun. We started writing our book—*An Alternative Lifestyle* and the newsletter got fancier. It went from two pages to five and our "subscription" list grew to 50.

April found us heading toward Los Angeles, California, for the April 28 wedding of son Mark and his bride, Ana. On the way we visited more family in New Mexico and Arizona.

Right after the wedding, we headed back to Michigan with a short stop in Las Vegas. We were back by May 17 and stayed in Michigan until the middle of September. Most of our camping in June and July was in family driveways. We attended four family reunions, camped with the granddaughters, attended several high school graduations, and celebrated the wedding of our good friends—Jim and Norma.

Most of the month of August was spent exploring Michigan's Upper Peninsula. We sent out applications for volunteer positions at two national parks and two national forests, in the mid south, for the months of October and November, so we could easily get back to Michigan for the December 1 wedding of daughter Susie to Ross Curtiss. We received replies from all and accepted positions at Hot Springs National Park in Arkansas. We worked on the book some and the newsletter got real fancy—we added photos.

October and November in Arkansas were wonderful. The climate was near-perfect. Their mountains were full of color. Yes, we would consider settling down there someday. Who knows? We loved our volunteer work and spent five days a week in the visitor center helping in many ways. We led tours, developed a computer program to expedite scheduling and worked the information desk. We liked it so much that we applied to six parks in the southwest, for the months of February to June. Where we go next depends on the responses. If there are none, we will just frog around in the southwest (Texas, Arizona, California) until the coast is clear (winter weather is gone) before heading northwest. We have a lot of sightseeing to do.

Guess we don't need to tell you that we still really love this lifestyle. We have met so many wonderful people, seen so much of this country, and know that we have only scratched the surface. As we circle the country and come into your area, you can be sure that we will give you a call. It would be nice if we could get together for a while. Write when you get a chance. We love mail. **MERRY CHRISTMAS!!!!**

From The May 1992 Issue of Movin' On

MOM H FALLS IN LOVE WITH TEXAS

Ron's Mom, Elsie Hofmeister from Winter Haven, Florida, has a weakness for elder hostels and likes to plan one in conjunction with a family visit if possible. Elder hostels are for those who are young at heart, but over 60 years of age. It is usually a week long event often held at a university, and includes classes and tours on one or several subjects. She picked the Texas History hostel which was held in Austin on the campus of the University of Texas, March 2 to March 6. Ron and Barb asked her to stay a week after her classes so they could show her around.

Part of the hostel program was a trip to the LBJ Ranch. They knew which day she was coming and asked their supervisors if there was any way they could be scheduled to work and actually drive her tour bus. Although it meant juggling the schedule some, Sally Armstrong pulled it off.

Barb was the bus driver that day and was at the Visitor Center early to greet the tour group. She made sure that Elsie got the front seat on the right of the bus—a special seat. The first stop on the tour was the LBJ birthplace and Ron was the guide there. As the group walked up to the home and son and mother recognized each other, both beamed and took time out for hugs before the presentation was made. Elsie said she was so proud of both her son and daughter-in-law and felt like a celebrity for the remainder of the classes at her hostel. Everyone asked her questions about Ron and Barb's lifestyle and so on.

Ron picked his mom up at the university at the close of the hostel and brought her out to the ranch. She was a good sport and spent the first night in the motorhome with the couple. She got a kick out of the cows looking in at them all the time and enjoyed an early morning walk to get a close look at some of the other wild life at the ranch.

Saturday the 7th, they packed suitcases and went to the Summit CCC at Canyon Lake where they had rented a little log cabin. Their thinking was it would be more comfortable with more room. It was too primitive though and really less comfortable than the motorhome. But the four days there weren't wasted. They spent Sunday afternoon at Barb's Aunt Genevieve's house in Austin where she prepared a delicious dinner. Cousin Mary and her husband Bill were there too.

Good friends of the Hofmeisters, Ed & Laurie Waples, live at

Canyon Lake and they took the trio on a first class tour of San Antonio which included the missions, the River Walk and then a trolley ride to the marketplace.

Another day the trio visited *New Braunfels* and *Gruene*. Gruene was especially fun because of the interesting old buildings and the general store where they sat at the counter and ordered ice cream cones.

They moved back to the LBJ Ranch on Wednesday, the 11th and spent two nights there. From that location, they visited *Fredricksburg* and included a delicious German dinner at the Bavarian Inn. A good part of another day was spent visiting the *Admiral Nimitz Museum* also in Fredricksburg. It details his life and WWII in the Pacific. At the ranch, Elsie had fun just relaxing and enjoying the cattle and the fresh air. While at the ranch, they also visited the famous town of Lukenbach and Ron took his Mom to the living history farm which is a part of the LBJ State park.

On Friday the 13th, they packed suitcases again and went to *The Ranch* CCC in Spicewood (northwest of Austin). On the way (well just a little out of the way), they visited the *Bluebonnet Cafe* in *Marble Falls* for lunch. Barb says they have wonderful pies and she

should know.

The stone cabin at The Ranch was clean, spacious, pleasantly rustic, comfortable and afforded the most breathtaking views of Lake Travis. The kitchen was complete with every tool, pans, dishes and included a micro wave.

Saturday evening, Liz and Don Ryding (volunteers at the LBJ Ranch) came out for dinner. Elsie had known the Rydings from when Don's brother was her minister many years ago. After dinner, they had fun playing dominoes.

During the day at The Ranch, they listened to the birds, music on tape, played games, talked, read, walked and just soaked up the relaxation of it all.

Elsie said it was a wonderful vacation. She got to see the beginnings of the Bluebonnets blooming, and got a hint of why Ron and Barb love the Hill Country so. Every time they were out riding, she wondered where every one was. Unlike Florida, there is no traffic.

Ron said, "It was fun to share our lifestyle with her, and I loved seeing her enjoy new things. And the very best of all, I didn't have to go to Florida."

The couple hopes she will come again next year when the wild flowers are out.

♥ ⌂ ♥

3

WHAT SHOULD WE LIVE IN?

This has been a difficult chapter to write. How can one advise another on what type of home they should have? Like traditional homes, RV selection depends on individual needs and tastes. There are many considerations that will affect the choice of an RV for full-timing. If you are comfortable with an RV that you have been using for vacations or weekend excursions, consider it for full-timing—especially if it's paid for. Not only is it economical to do this, it allows time to gain experience on the road. Remember we call experience an adventure. Additional needs and experience will enter into

27

making a wise RV selection when upgrading later.

If buying a new RV, consider some optional equipment. When made part of the original deal their inclusion can be less expensive. Optional equipment could include air conditioning, a roof storage pod, solar panels, awnings, special television antennas, valve extenders, black water flush system or perhaps a washer and dryer. In the case of motorhomes,

European Full-timer

one could add a closed circuit television monitor for backing, hydraulic levelers, and generators. If all of these goodies are not in the current RV this should not be a deterrent. Accessories can be added later or incorporated into a new RV if, and when, the RV home is upgraded.

Even the most basic RV will have a refrigerator, freezer, hot water heater, dinette, stove, oven, toilet, shower and a small kitchen. Sleeping arrangements range from a bed which is permanently made up to a dinette or couch that converts to a bed. Almost all class C type motorhomes have a bed over the cab area. All RVs have separate holding tanks for black water (sewage), grey water (sink/shower), and storage tanks for fresh water and propane gas. Electrical energy is provided to the RV by an electrical connection for outside sources and a storage battery or generator when electricity is not available. Most RVs are set up for 20/30 amps while the very large models use 50 amps. Inside and outside storage areas will vary with manufacturer and model. So, even without optional equipment, the basic RV may provide enough comfort for the beginning full-timer.

Quite by accident our first motorhome had jalousie windows. We did not specify them. They are wonderful on a hot, humid, rainy day, because we can open the windows without it raining in. Now we wouldn't be without them. We have found there are other important features of an RV of which potential full-timers should be aware. No matter how well one plans there will be times (even in Florida) when cold weather will have to be dealt with. During these times, a well insulated RV will take a big load off of the heating system, and propane usage ($) will be lower. Exposed holding tanks can also freeze during a prolonged period of below freezing weather. Although, there are ways of dealing with this when in a site with full hookups, it is less worrisome if the RV has an enclosed, heated area for holding tanks and plumbing lines. The size of fresh water tanks, waste water holding tanks, hot water heater, gasoline tank(s), and propane tanks are important too. But, when planning to use full hookups often, the need for large fresh water and waste holding tanks is less critical.

The price range of the RV will usually determine the size of holding tanks. If planning on a lot of dry camping, it's best to give these items serious consideration. We have found that a six gallon hot water heater is more than adequate because of its rapid recovery, and it is standard on most lower and medium priced RVs. With careful use, the 30-40 gallon black water holding tank, found on many lower priced RVs, need only be emptied once a week. The grey water holding tank, however, usually has to be emptied at least twice a week.

It's apparent that equipment and special features will play an important part in the selection of an RV. When considering an especially good buy, it's comforting to know that equipment, such as air conditioners and awnings, can be added later.

When we purchased our Bounder motorhome, at Lazy Days RV Center in Tampa, Florida, we were very impressed with the work they do in making RVs handicap accessible. They devote two of their 48 service bays to modifying RVs for the handicapped. They have specially trained technicians whose primary responsibility is to revise RVs for those with special needs so they can enjoy this lifestyle too.

So, what type of RV works best for full-timing? Quite frankly, our experience has been limited to motorhomes, and our biases will probably come through in this chapter. It's a rare campground, however, where full-timers don't get together and discuss their "homes." We have enjoyed these discussions and have learned a lot from them. Some have found that their requirements changed with different periods in their lives. The following discussion is not meant to be all inclusive, but it may generate some ideas.

Travel Trailers

If planning on staying several months in one location and taking advantage of monthly rates or climate, a travel trailer could be an economical choice. Depending on size of unit and skill of the driver, however, a travel trailer may be cumbersome when moving often. Set-up and backing can be stressful for some people. On the plus side, however, the towing vehicle (suburban, van or pickup) is available for local area driving. Most travel trailers are less expensive to purchase and maintain in comparison with motorhomes or fifth-wheels.

Travel Trailer and Tow Vehicle

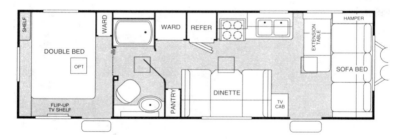

Figure 1 *Wilderness Travel Trailer — Model 27G*

Travel trailers offer good living space. There are many floor plans, but generally the bedroom is in the back with the kitchen either in the center or in front. Travel trailers are nicely decorated, have adequate closet and cupboard space, but outside storage space is very limited. This is a deterrent for many full-timers. Although, when comparing a 27-foot trailer (Fig.1) with a 27-foot class C motor home (Fig.4), it's easy to see the difference in floor space. In a motorhome for example, some of what could be living space is taken up with the driving area and the engine. Travel trailers seem more like a home to many people, because it is separate from the vehicle that pulls it. Because of this, a stop at a picnic area for lunch, will involve exiting the towing vehicle and then entering the trailer. This is only a problem in bad weather.

Fifth-wheels

Fifth-wheels are similar to trailers, except that a portion of the trailer extends over the bed of a pickup truck. It operates

30' Fifth Wheel and Conventional Tow Vehicle

in concert with the pickup, similar to a semi-tractor trailer. Most agree that road handling and backing with a fifth-wheel is much easier than a travel trailer. However, certain skills are needed, and the set up is similar to a travel trailer. Here

Figure 2 *Wilderness Fifth Wheel — Model 27 5N*

again, the towing vehicle can be used for local travel while the main unit is parked. But, the towing vehicle is usually a heavy duty, high-powered pickup truck that may not be fuel efficient when used for local area travel. Like the travel trailer, fifth-wheels are usually less expensive than motorhomes and, because of their design, provide a lot of space for the money. Fifth-wheels have more outside storage than the travel trailer,

An Unusual Towing Vehicle and Workshop Combination

but not as much as the larger motorhomes.

To us, the inside of the fifth-wheel trailer is even more like a home. First of all, the front of the trailer, which fits over the bed of the truck when traveling, is higher than the rest of the trailer. Inside, there will be several steps up to that area. The steps nicely separate that area (usually the bedroom and bathroom) from the rest of the house. This makes for more privacy. Closets are roomy and tall especially in the area just before the steps to the upper level. Many have beautiful roomy cabinets, and the rear kitchen, with a free standing table and chairs, seems to have the most counter space. Like the trailer, there is no engine area to take away from living space.

Figure 3 *Wilderness Fifth Wheel — Model 27 5J*

A favorite feature which is almost standard on many fifth-wheels now is the "slide out" or "tip out." Once parked, the slide out is pulled out (hydraulically) and the room/rooms become wider. Then it really looks and feels like a home. We have seen 40-foot fifth-wheels with three slide outs (kitchen, living room and bedroom) complete with washer/dryer, dishwasher and more living space than many apartments. Of course these are not easily moved into a national park site or even some of the commercial campgrounds. But there are many moderate sized fifth-wheel trailers with slide outs that are just right for full-timers.

One of the benefits of owning a travel trailer or fifth-wheel is that there is no engine in the house. If a tuneup or oil change is needed, it is not necessary to take in the whole house.

Motorhomes

Motorhomes are luxurious to travel with and are comfortable to live in. The deluxe cockpit and console, in close proximity to all the conveniences of a modern kitchen and

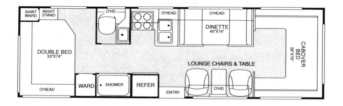

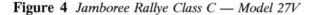

Figure 4 *Jamboree Rallye Class C — Model 27V*

bathroom, make travel a delight. Motorhomes can range from $10,000 (for a ten year old used model) to $500,000 or more for a luxurious bus type land cruiser used by entertainers and a select few full-timers. Many fine motorhomes fall in the $30,000—$75,000 range. Most people find motorhomes easy to drive and maneuver in the campground. Class A motorhomes are those where the complete body is constructed by the RV manufacturer with the truck manufacturer supplying the chassis and engine. The driver area is open and part of the front living area. A class C motorhome utilizes the cab furnished by the truck manufacturer. The RV manufacturer then modifies it to include a space over the driver and passenger area (usually a loft type bed). The rest of the motorhome is then constructed on the truck manufacturers chassis by the RV manufacturer. The large motorhomes are often powered by diesel engines on a heavy duty chassis. For the weight that they push, they are surprisingly fuel efficient. They are called diesel pushers because the engine is in the rear. Many are bus type rigs and the chassis, engine and shell are supplied to the RV manufacturer by those firms manufacturing large buses.

Motorhomes are quite roomy and can have good storage and closet space. Outside storage is a plus for motorhomes, especially with the many "basement" models now on the market.

Some motorhomes look like living room and kitchen, then convert into bedrooms at bedtime. The couch and dinettes both make into beds. The class C motorhome also has the cab-over bed. This is OK for the occasional trip, but a daily dose of this type of bed is no fun. In many of the smaller motorhomes, the manufacturers tuck in a bed along the rear curbside wall. It is difficult at best to make, because there is no area to walk around. The only way it can be made up is by

Our First Motorhome—24' Class C

sitting on the bed. This, again, is OK for weekends, but not for everyday living. Many RVers choose the Class C model and sleep on the cab over bed, but it is no easier to make,

Motorhome and Tow Vehicle

and someone has to sleep against the wall and crawl over their partner to get out of bed. The best motorhome choice, in our opinion, is one long enough for a couch and chair in the area behind the driver, a dinette near the kitchen area,

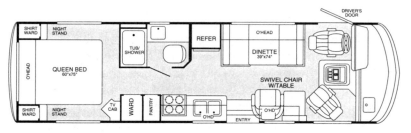

Figure 5 *Southwind Motorhome Model 29F*

and a full walk around bed in the rear.

We have mentioned the comfort of a motorhome at travel

time. In bad weather, stops are no problem. Before full-timing, we were making a spring trip to New Mexico and came upon very icy conditions in the Panhandle of Texas. We simply pulled off the road, ate breakfast in the comfort of our home and relaxed until the sun melted the ice.

Towed Vehicles for Motorhomes

It is advisable to tow a small car or pickup behind the motor home. After a motor home is leveled and set up at the campsite, it is not convenient to unhook and drive it into town for groceries or to go sight seeing. It is also expensive since most motorhomes are not fuel efficient. Our motorhome only travels from point to point and then only for short distances. Gasoline is not a major part of our budget. During our first year of full-timing, the motorhome traveled approximately 10,000 miles, even though we traveled through twenty-five states. On the other hand, our little tow vehicle, which averaged 35 miles per gallon, recorded 30,000 miles including the 10,000 towed miles. Imagine all those miles on a high powered pickup used to tow a travel trailer or fifth-wheel. In our opinion, the opportunity to tow a small vehicle for vicinity travel is the biggest advantage of using a motorhome for full-timing.

Towing a small vehicle is not normally a problem. Connections have been made simple with self storing or easily detached tow bars. Most drivers feel that the car is hardly noticeable when towed behind the motorhome. If a car is towed on all four wheels it must have a manual transmission unless certain mechanical adjustments are made. Some manufacturers do not recommend that their cars be towed on all four wheels. An alternative is a tow dolly or a trailer. Towing trailers or dollies may or may not have braking capabilities, but the odometer of the car being towed is not recording miles. The disadvantages are that the dolly or trailer must be stored at the campsite where space is often limited. Also, the hookup of car and trailer can be difficult and time consuming.

The best vehicle to tow depends on personal preference and the capabilities of the motorhome. A gasoline powered motorhome will function best, towing a smaller unit. However, we have seen the large diesels towing such large cars as a Lincoln Town Car. The RV manufacturer is the best source of information as to the towing capabilities of it's product. A popular full-timer towed vehicle is the small, light weight, half ton, pickup truck with a cap covering the bed of the truck. The obvious advantage is the added storage. We elected to go this route when we had a smaller motorhome. But with plenty of basement storage now, we feel that we would like to go back to a small car. There have been many times when we would have liked to take friends or family on short trips but had to take separate vehicles. Our fellow volunteers at the LBJ Ranch had the same problem. When we went out to dinner together, we each drove our pickups.

What are the most popular towing methods? Our observations, both on the road and in campgrounds, are that towing small vehicles on all four wheels is most popular. Like others, we find it more convenient and economical and have mastered the hookup time to less than five minutes. When arriving at a campground, it only takes a minute to disconnect and temporarily hook the tow bar to an upright position on the car. This allows immediate freedom to park the car and maneuver the motorhome into the campsite. If concerned about mileage being recorded on the odometer while towing, there is a disconnect available through Remco Inc. Their toll-free number is 1-800-228-2481. When the car in tow is connected to the motor home, mileage is not recorded. *Motorhome* magazine devoted a major portion of it's March 1990 issue to the mechanics of towing vehicles behind motorhomes, including manufacturers recommendations. They now run a yearly update on dinghy towing, as it is called.

Our cost of conversion for towing was about $350 and included a tow bar, bumper connections, and electrical connections. On most small vehicles the installer will have to weld base plates where the bumpers attach to the frame. This is not uncommon on small vehicles with unibody construction. Our conversion cost did not include the motorhome hitch which is standard on many models. Costs of trailers and dollies vary widely, however, it is possible to purchase a good tow dolly for about $1,500.

RV Accessories

Once a "home" for full-timing has been selected, it's necessary to give thought as to how it's to be equipped. Your pocket book and personal preference will enter into these decisions; however, we have found that there are several options or accessories that are essential to full-timing. We have said that our back yard is the whole country, but it sure is nice to cover a little bit of that with an awning. It actually gives an extended living room feeling to the RV. Although it provides shade and even helps to keep the RV cool, we enjoy it more when it's raining. Our picnic table is usually under the awning. If the rain isn't blowing in, we can sit under it and have even eaten outside during a light rain. Number one accessory on our list, then, is the awning. There's even an addition to the awning that is available. It is a screen that zippers all around the awning and the entry side of the RV. This gives the feeling of a sunroom or porch and keeps insects away.

When we purchased our first motorhome, we opted for a roof air conditioner, even though we weren't sure we would use it that much. We reasoned that it would be better to have it factory installed, and it would help the resale value of the motorhome if we ever decided to sell. Our thoughts have changed about air conditioners. Even if you don't like them there are times when they are essential. More and more we are finding ourselves in warmer weather. Frequently, we find that it's necessary to close up the RV due to bugs, particularly the tiny "no-see-ums" that come right through the screens. During those times, we were happy to have air conditioning. We probably use the fan feature of the air conditioning more than the air itself. It's handy to have. Most large RV's have two units and our new motorhome is no exception. In order to avoid direct air cooling, we find it helpful to operate the unit in the unoccupied part of the RV. It's hard to imagine a full-time rig without an air conditioning unit.

Many people consider their generator as their most important accessory and include a factory installed one in their original purchase. Others, pick up a portable generator after they have been on the road a while. And still others would not have one under any circumstance. Anti-generator campers object to the noise of a generator, particularly in the quiet setting of a remote national park. Several chapters could be written on the pros and cons of generators. Although, we rarely use a generator, we enjoy the security of having one. We feel that it adds to the value of our rig and we like the fact that it was part of the original equipment. There will be times when we will need it, and it gives us some attractive alternatives. It's no secret that the large rigs have a lot of electrical equipment on board, including computers, printers, air conditioners, microwave ovens, gas detectors, automatic ignitors, and the list goes on. Ignitors and gas detectors need to operate, even when dry camping. An hour or two a day will keep the batteries charged and allow the RV to function properly. Even if you never dry camp, dealers advise owners of large motorhomes to operate the roof air while traveling, and a generator will allow you to do this. They maintain that using the generator to operate the roof air requires less energy and takes the strain off of the cab air conditioning. While using the roof air, the fuel usage will actually be lower and it will be more comfortable.

Almost everyone has a television antenna; however, on

some RV models they are not standard equipment. It is best to include a factory installed antenna, if only for resale value. Although we rarely watch television, there have been rainy days when it came in handy, and on events of national importance we want to know what is going on. These include World Series games, Super Bowl and the Olympic Games. We have noticed small satellite dishes on top of RVs, particularly the luxury bus type motorhomes. Even these are not necessary in many campgrounds where cable TV is available.

Another helpful accessory is the panel that shows fluid levels and battery condition. This panel is standard equipment on most models and optional on others. Indicator lights on the panel show how full the holding tanks are, level of fresh water and the quantity of propane. Battery strength is shown as good, fair or poor. Happiness is having empty holding tanks, full fresh water and propane tanks and a fully charged battery.

When first full-timing in a small motorhome, we found it hard to imagine other full-timers, in the same sized motorhome, without a roof storage pod. We called it our attic and selected the largest one available. If a pod is needed, it should be selected in consultation with, and installed by, a qualified RV dealer. It is necessary to be aware of manufacturer's limitations on the roof and to have proper sealing where the unit is attached to the RV. Since it's on the roof, it's best to store items that are not used frequently. Items stored in our "attic" were winter clothes, lantern, tennis rackets, rain gear, decorative lights, a one foot tall decorated Christmas tree, and plastic air mattresses for lounging in pools. We also stored flat, soft type luggage, fishing gear, a small cooler and golf clubs. Larger RVs—especially the basement model motorhomes, do not need pods.

Some motorhome owners feel the need for automatic levelers, even though they are very expensive. They are often standard equipment in the luxury models, but whether standard or optional, they add between $3,000 and $4,000 dollars to the cost of the unit. There were times during our first years that we dreamed of someday owning a motorhome with automatic levelers. This was especially true when we were blocking up the front wheels with every board we had in order to be passably level in sister Linda's steep downhill driveway. Some may be able to adjust their sleeping habits to a downhill slope, but their refrigerator will insist that it be somewhat level in order to operate properly. In most public and private campgrounds the sites are within one or two boards of being level, and in many, boards are not necessary at all. We used to envy those who pulled into a campground and could level their unit while still sitting in the driver's seat by pushing a few levers. Now we know that joy. By the way, being able to add levelers is a fringe benefit of having a motorhome. Travel trailers and fifth-wheels do not have this option.

The list of options is long and sometimes expensive, and we have just mentioned a few major ones. Full-timers generally have lots of time and actually enjoy expending the effort that some of the accessories eliminate. As noted in the above discussion, though, there are several that every full timer should seriously consider.

Making a Decision

After narrowing down the type of RV, it is now time to investigate different models and floor plans. When looking for an RV, take the time to sit on the sofa, while the spouse tries to walk past. While pretending to work in the kitchen area, see if there is room for someone to pass. Check out the bathroom. See if the bed will be easy to make and so on. A little extra time taken before the purchase, will add to the joy on the road. Negotiate for special furnishings in the RV. For example, if interested in an RV with a free standing table and chairs rather than the dinette, ask. But if you do change to a free standing table, you will lose valuable storage space. These are things to think about. At any rate, the big RV dealers will go out of their way to accommodate their customers.

In addition to livability, it is extremely important to consider weight. Every RV has its weight limitations and they are often violated. It is tempting, especially by full-timers, to overload. The fact that storage space is available does not necessarily mean that weight can be added. Some models provide very little margin for extra weight, and even the weight of the passengers will preclude adding anything else. Every purchaser will want to check the manufacturer's published weight loads. They are required to list them in the vehicle and in their literature. UVW (unloaded vehicle weight) is the weight of the vehicle with maximum capacity of all fluids necessary for the operation of the vehicle, but without cargo, occupants or accessories that are ordinarily removed from the vehicle when it is not in use. GVWR (gross vehicle weight rating) is the maximum weight that the vehicle is designed to carry. Likewise, there are ratings for the front axle (GAWR-F) and the rear axle (GAWR-R). The difference between the unloaded weight and the maximum allowable should allow for passengers, fluids, supplies and belongings. Do not assume that the manufacturer provides ample capacity—some do not. It is also best to weigh each axle and side to insure proper loading. An improperly loaded RV can cause axle damage, severe tire wear and, in some cases, engine and transmission damage. Most of the well known manufacturers are careful to design a functional RV, but full-timers have special needs. They should be addressed up front in the RV selection.

So what RV is best for full-timing? All have pluses and minuses. Like us, your decision will depend on personal preference and pocketbook. Let us recap.

Travel trailers are less expensive and provide a lot of interior room for the money. There is little, if any, outside storage and handling may be a problem.

Fifth-wheels also provide a lot of interior room for the money and have more storage. They are a little easier to handle than the travel trailer, but they cost more. Both travel trailer and fifth-wheel require that the large towing vehicle be used for vicinity mileage. Unless the pickup is one of the newer super cabs, it can be uncomfortable if a lot of time is spent traveling. Several full-timers, that we have met, solved this problem by taking along a small car. The large towing truck is seldom unhooked from the trailer. The car is driven separately to their next destination. This may be all right, if the plan is to stay put for long periods of time. It seems, to us, like a lonesome way to travel.

We selected a motor home for four reasons: (1) we already owned one (the best reason of all); (2) we expected to be continually on the move; (3) we like to travel in comfort when we are on the move; and (4) the availability of a small tow car for vicinity driving.

We have met many full-timers who are very satisfied with their particular choice of RV and wouldn't consider changing. It's fun to explore the different choices and exciting to finally move into the new home.

♥   ♥

From The December 1990 Issue Of Movin' On

WE ARE HOME

When Brenda and Judy visited us in Hot Springs recently, it was their second vacation in a month. One trip to visit a friend in Tennessee kept them gone over a week. When they stopped in HS, they were on their way to visit relatives in Dallas, Texas, and were going to be gone for nearly two weeks again. They were tired of traveling and longed to be home. In their frustration, they asked us if we ever just want to "go home?" Our answer was that we are always home. We take our home with us. Think about it!

We never have to worry about hotel rooms, lumpy, hard or soft mattresses—we have our own wonderful bed, pillows, comforter—no matter where we go. We have closets with clothes always hanging ready to wear. We even carry our refrigerator and stove and cupboards with us. How often do you get that in a motel? I can fix popcorn at a moment's notice or whip up an elegant meal. We also have our books, games, and computer with us.

We don't have to ride elevators to get to our room, nor do we have to listen to cars zooming by on the freeway beside the motel. We have a bar, music, TV, an excellent restaurant complete with charcoal grill, and we don't have to wait more than ten minutes to get our coffee in the morning; nor do we have to get dressed to go out and get it.

After our trip to Michigan this month, I can appreciate their frustration. I can't wait to get back home. Home is our motorhome parked at Gulpha Gorge Campground in Hot Springs, Arkansas, (until we move it somewhere else). **It is home and we love it dearly.**

From the January 1993 issue of Movin' On

A NEW HOME
For The Hofmeisters

Ron and Barb had been sold on the Bounder motorhome in January of last year when they attended an RV show in Tucson, Arizona, but they weren't ready to buy at that time. They kept talking about "maybe" looking at motorhomes when they finished their volunteer work at the LBJ ranch this next May.

The Hofmeisters were camped in Kissimmee, Florida, and struck up a conversation with a couple camped nearby. Fred and Doris Davis, full-timers from the west coast, had just picked up their new Bounder from LazyDays RV sales in Tampa, Florida. They had purchased it over the phone—from California—and drove cross country to make the trade. They said that no one could beat the deal from LazyDays. That impressed the Hofmeisters, and for a minute they talked about driving over to Tampa when they were camping in Lakeland to "just look." They dismissed that idea. It would be too much torture since they still weren't ready to buy.

A few days later, when they pulled into the CC Campground in Lakeland, they were told that the park was having an RV show and to be sure and browse through the models. Since they were right there, Barb convinced Ron that it was harmless to look. One of the models on display was a 34' Bounder and it seemed so big to Barb. Ron asked for a price after trade in, and it was better than he thought it would be. He started doing some figuring and later suggested they take the short drive to Tampa to see what kind of price LazyDays could come up with.

LazyDays has to be the largest RV dealer in the world just from the size of their lots—one each for motorhomes, trailers, bus conversions and used RVs. Salesman, Pat Overby, was very helpful and he took plenty of time to show the couple Bounders and other similar motorhomes. They discussed used coaches, diesel vs gas engines, hydraulic levelers, awnings, back up camera, and made a deal on a 1993, 34-foot Ford Chassis Bounder with all of the luxuries except a horn to play "On the Road Again." The Bounder they wanted was not in stock, but Pat promised it would be there by Dec 1.

Both Barb and Ron remarked that this was the most relaxed buying experience ever. "There was no pressure and everything was handled very professionally and speedily," said Ron. Just as promised, the motorhome was indeed ready. In fact Ron and Barb received a call on Saturday, November 28, saying the coach was in. Monday morning early they left West Palm Beach and drove to Tampa arriving at close to four p.m.

Barb explained, "We figured we were too late to take delivery that day, but we hoped they would let us park in the lot anyway. You see, there was a Kinkos Copy Center just down the road and I wanted to get the December newsletter printed and out before we started moving. We were told to check in at the main office and when we did, we were greeted by our salesman Pat, and the credit gal, Lori. In less than one half hour, all the papers were signed and the house was ours. They told us they would park us next to the Bounder and we could move in at our convenience. They added that we could take as much time as we needed. It was a beautiful surprise."

By six p.m., the two motorhomes were parked side by side in the service lot, and the gates were locked for the night. The security couple came to say, "hello," and mentioned that if there was anything they could do to help, just to holler. At first Barb and Ron just looked at their new home with awe. They would get the walk through in the morning, but in the meantime, they just opened cupboards and drawers and languished in all the room. Ron sat on the couch then one of the chairs and back on the couch. His eyes were looking up at the blank TV screen. "This is gonna be great. I can lay here and watch football games." Barb groaned, but turned on the TV so he could have the full effect.

Barb's thoughts were about how nice it was going to be to walk to the bedroom or bathroom and actually close a door; and she would be able to keep the computer set up and not affect dinner at the dinette.

After a while, they put their comfort on hold and started moving. Barb wasn't sure where to begin. Since she hadn't been able to make a bed without sitting on it for the last 3½ years, she opted to make the bed first. "It's like a bed in a house," she exclaimed, "I can walk around it." Deciding where to put things was somewhat of a problem although Barb commented that she had been "moving mentally" all that month so she had a pretty good idea where everything could go. "Having so much cupboard and outside storage space is like heaven," she added.

Ron moved goods into the outside compartments and carried baskets full of things into the Bounder while Barb put things away inside. At one time Ron was heard to holler, "Where did all this stuff come from? We must have been overweight." As Barb was putting it away she too wondered where it had all been stashed.

At 10 p.m., they took a break to deliver the newsletter to Kinkos. Instead of waiting for it to be printed, they made arrangements to pick it up the next day. There was more moving to do. Finally at midnight, Ron and Barb pulled the shades and fell into bed exhausted. The first night in their new home.

Their "move in coordinator," Bill, spent about 1½ hours doing the walk through with the Hofmeisters the next morning. They learned about the two furnaces, two air conditioners, the hydraulic leveling jacks, awnings (1 patio & 4 window), two televisions, built in VCR, microwave, water filter system, back up camera, water and sewer hookups, 7000 Onan generator and all the storage compartments.

The rest of the day was spent between moving, folding newsletters, and taking a tour of the facility. Barb wanted to know all about this efficient and very successful business. She was most fascinated by the 48 service bays some of which are very specialized. For example, two bays and a team of specialists are devoted to just making RVs handicap accessible. The couple saw some horribly mangled RVs which were being re-built and one whose repair was just completed. After hurricane Andrew and a local tornado, the service department had had some major repair jobs.

Barb was especially impressed with the 40 X 20 training room where walls were plastered with 10 large customer service signs. Their motto covers a large outside wall:

"To make sure that our customers feel so good about the product that they bought and their decision to buy from us that they become our customers for life."

After spending a week in Winter Haven, they went back to LazyDays to get some minor warranty work done and were again treated like someone special. Although it took three days to get the necessary part for the furnace (new model year parts weren't in stock), Ron and Barb were camped in comfort in a service bay right next to the customer lounge and lots of fresh coffee. They understood that normally there is a hostess there who makes and serves fresh sticky buns each morning. She has been in Miami since Andrew though. LazyDays set up an office there to help house the homeless. Ron and Barb weren't the only ones "camped" in the service lot either time. Others were moving from motorhome to motorhome and 5th wheel to 5th wheel and so on. After all, the company sells approximately 250 units a month and services about 30 units a day.

Barb wondered how Ron would feel driving the monster, and he surprised her by taking to it like a duck to water. Barb detailed the driving experience. "The night we left Tampa—the first time—and headed to Winter Haven, it seemed to get dark fast and we were on a curvy, two lane road with no shoulder. He drove it like it was nothing and all the while I was thinking that I couldn't have done that. He made me drive it on our way to Texas and I have to admit it isn't that much different from our Mallard Sprinter. Actually it is stranger being the passenger. If I walk all the way back to the bedroom, I can't see Ron. He can't see me either because of the side aisle design; and, it is so long."

Ron commented, "It doesn't take long to get used to luxury."

♥ ⌂ ♥

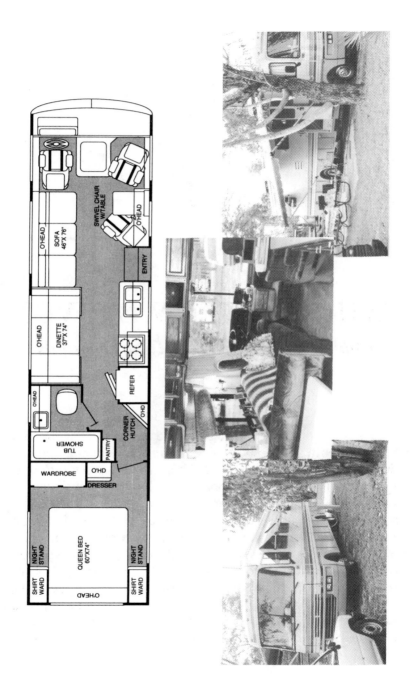

4

WHERE WILL WE LIVE?

Public & Commercial Campgrounds

Living on the road is similar, in two respects, to living in a house. In both situations, it depends on where people want to live and what they can afford. There are so many different approaches and combinations of methods to full-timing, it would take another book to list them all. We will discuss some of the most common approaches and leave it to the reader's inventiveness to come up with the method or combination that is best for them. In Chapter 10, you will see that our budget for campground fees is $175 per month. In order to stay within this figure, we have used a variety of methods.

The type of camping that is covered in this and the next two chapters include the following: public campgrounds (national, state, county and municipal parks), commercial campgrounds (overnight and long term), private membership parks, boondocking (free), campground hosting or volunteering, and public dry camping (not really campgrounds, however a small fee may be required).

Federal, State, County & Municipal Campgrounds

There's no doubt that by using our country's beautiful network of public parks, it's possible to budget modestly for campground fees. We love the parks and include them in our itinerary as often as possible. As mentioned in Chapter 1, it is our goal to visit all of the national parks in the continental United States.

If national parks are in the plan, be prepared to rough it, since most do not have hookups or showers. The rest rooms in most national park campgrounds do not even have hot water. By conserving water and energy, we find that we can get along fine for a week without hookups. But that means water efficient showers or sponge baths and charging our battery in the day time with our generator. Many full-timers prefer to use generators while some may use only solar panels or a combination of solar power and a small generator. Assuming full-timers will not be spending a great deal of time in cold weather, electrical energy needs should not be great unless addicted to television, microwave oven, toasters, curling irons and the like.

No matter how well we plan, there are times when we get caught in cold weather. When that happens, the sweaters come out, and whatever energy we can generate is reserved for the furnace. Those experienced in dry camping have catalytic heaters and well-insulated rigs. Some may go to bed early and snuggle under a down comforter. The cold usually lasts for only a few days, but even in the deepest part of the Sunbelt, occasional cold snaps occur. If it looks like it will last more than a couple of days, one can head for a full hookup.

That way a portable electric heater and/or furnace may be used. Even though the furnace operates on propane, the fan uses a lot of electrical energy. The 12 volt house batteries in most RVs will run down after a few hours of furnace operation. Solar panels and small generators are not capable of putting that much energy back into the battery. When we were campground hosts at Yosemite National Park, one spring, we struggled to keep warm. The April day time temperatures stayed in the low to mid 40's, and we did not have electricity. We thought we could manage with the 600-watt generator we added to our 24-foot Class C motorhome, but we found that we could only run our furnace for a quick warm up in the morning and once again before going to bed. Every other day or so, we had to run the generator four hours to recharge our house battery. We kept warm by staying near a constant campfire and wearing lots of warm clothing. A catalytic heater would have been a Godsend to us and is something to look into if you plan on being where the temperatures will stay on the cold side.

We are grateful that most of the parks have dump stations. In our travels we have found many state parks with both water and electricity, but most have just electricity. On occasion, it's possible to find hookups in a national park when the national park has taken over a former state park or when a concessionaire provides them. Municipal and county parks run the gamut of services, and some are outstanding in addition to being reasonably priced.

Federally owned parks include not only national parks, but national forest campgrounds (very rustic), Corps of Engineer campgrounds (usually by dam sites) and national monuments. Generally, the more primitive—the more scenic. Primitive is fun when on vacation, but a steady diet of dry camping can place a strain on full-timers. We like to mix it up. When camping in public parks, the size of an RV is often critical. Most of the remote national forest campgrounds, and even some national parks, would not be accessible to a rig over 32 feet long. Sometimes a 24-foot rig would have trouble getting in. A 40-foot fifth-wheel or motor home? Forget it!

If either spouse is age 62 or older, he/she is eligible for the federal "Golden Age" pass which entitles holders to half-price rates for camping and free park entrance fees. At Gulf Islands National Seashore Park in Ocean Springs, Mississippi, we found that we were the only ones in the campground paying more than the half price rate of $6 a night because neither of us was 62. But even at $12, we thought the campground was a bargain because we had water, electricity and modern showers in a beautiful park setting.

Liberally adding national park visits to the itinerary can add to the full-timing enjoyment while reducing campground expense. Many states have state forest campgrounds similar to the national forest campgrounds. These primitive campgrounds are usually self-registering, not assessable to large rigs, and offer a minimum of security. What they lack in facilities, they make up for in serenity and beauty. They are very inexpensive and should not be overlooked by those who enjoy nature and primitive camping.

Many state park systems have an unbeatable combination of beauty and amenities. They are also very affordable. For example, using their annual permit, Texas has many beautiful state parks with full hookups at $12 a night (1993 rate). However, many eastern states offer only dry camping, so it is best to consult the trusty campground directory when in this area. On the other hand, we were happy to discover the beautiful park system in Upper New York state with modern sites at modest prices. State park rates are usually in the $12 and below range (1993 rates), fitting into most full-timer's budgets. An exception to this is Florida and California, where even rustic sites are in the $15 and above range. For a time, Florida even charged nonresidents double (since rescinded). However, Florida does have a good national forest system and lots of good membership parks.

When camping in public parks, we find that we can operate

A Washington State Park Campsite

well with water and electricity, and if convenient to our RV, we use the public showers. Otherwise we use our own shower and dump the grey water at the dump station as needed. If not too far, we tote it in a large container. It may take several trips, but we have a lot of time.

Many ignore the municipal parks thinking they could not offer much. Not true! Many are equal to, or better than some of the other public parks. One we remember fondly is the Lady Bird Johnson Municipal Park in Fredricksburg, Texas. Situated in the beautiful Hill Country, the nicely landscaped campground is next to a challenging golf course. Tennis courts, fishing and a swimming pool round out the recreational extras. The location is a plus too—a few short miles from the charming German town of Fredricksburg.

In the busy season, most public parks have a 14-day

Lady Bird Johnson Municipal Park

limitation, but for us that is OK. By that time we are usually ready to move on. Since we have no time constraints or schedule, during the busy season, we try to move between parks early in the week. By Friday we are comfortably settled when the weekenders invade the parks. We smugly wave good-bye to them as they leave Sunday night so they can be back at work Monday morning. That brings up another favorite practice, namely, fall and spring camping in public parks. It's the best time. We love it when, except for one or two other full-timers, we have the campgrounds to ourselves. Even the Sunbelt states have their slow season and while it may be a little cool at times, we enjoy the solitude and beauty as we take a brisk morning walk.

Commercial Campgrounds

There are thousands of commercial campgrounds as evidenced in the large campground directories that look like big city telephone books. Geographical sections of the directories are available too. One of our favorites is *Trailer Life Campground & RV Service Directory*. It is inexpensive and available at a discount with Good Sam membership. Another good campground directory is *Woodalls*. Campground directories describe the campgrounds and give directions on how to get there. They list the type, number and width of spaces. Also listed are the amenities such as pool, store, laundry and miniature golf, and last year's rate. Some of the directories will rate the campground as to cleanliness and facilities. This is of particular interest when it comes to bathroom and shower facilities. That is one of the first things we look for as well as site width. We have seen site widths as narrow as 18 feet, and even though we are friendly people, we don't care to camp that close to our neighbor.

Not only do the major campground directories list commercial parks, they include public parks. They will describe the facilities, but will not apply their rating system to them. It's well to remember that the commercial campgrounds must pay and meet certain standards to be included in a directory. Because of that, there may be good campgrounds in an area that are not listed in the directories. Campground chains such as Kampgrounds of American (KOA) and Yogi Bear Jellystone Parks will supply directories of their own parks at no charge.

Commercial campgrounds come in many varieties. They vary as to size, character, amenities, purpose, and price. They may be seashore sites, ranches, overnight spots along an interstate highway, or a remote desert oasis. Some are five star resorts and others may be little more than an after thought or an appendage to an existing mobile home park or gas station. Full-timers will, at one time or another, use commercial campgrounds. They can be an important part of the overall operational plan and, surprisingly, can be cost effective.

We, like many full-timers, do not want to travel more than 200 miles a day. After all, what's the hurry? If moving to a new location that is farther than that, it's best to break up the trip. The campground directory can help locate convenient commercial parks along the major route. The price will probably be more than the average daily budget for campsites, but the convenience will be worth it. Many parks along major routes cater to the overnight traveler with excellent facilities that include clean rest rooms and showers, swimming pools, camp store and a propane outlet. Best of all, most of them have pull-throughs. This is very important because no one wants to unhook a tow car or trailer for one night.

While traveling in South Carolina, our traveling day ended on a positive note when we were able to pull into a KOA, register, fill up with propane, park in a pull-through and jump in the pool—all within 15 minutes. There are full-timers, however, who disagree with the use of overnight commercial parks. They feel that the $12 to $20 rates are too expensive. When stopping overnight, they prefer to boondock at highway rest areas, church parking lots, shopping center parking lots or any other place that will accommodate their rig. That is not our preference; however, it might work for others, and it certainly helps the budget. Speaking of budgets, full-timers recognize that even if they use commercial parks infrequently, a 10% discount can be obtained when the park accepts a Good Sam or a KOA card.

Commercial parks, with their amenities and desirable locations, can enrich the life of the full-timer. This is especially true in the winter. Many full-timers like to pull off the road for a month or two where they can depend on full hookups (in case of cold weather) and be with old friends during the holidays. Even in the most popular Sunbelt areas, monthly rates are usually affordable and often in the $200 range or less. This is particularly true along the Rio Grande Valley area in Texas. We have spent several months in Mission, Texas, and plan to visit again. There are thousands of RV sites in this area. The abundance of RV parks catering to "Snow Birds," keeps the rates competitive. The same is true in Florida, Arizona, and southern California. Since competition is keen, the parks go to great lengths to insure that their customers return every winter. Most offer craft lessons, potlucks, holiday get-togethers, shuffleboard, heated pools, dances, card parties, bingo and exercise classes. Some even have bus excursion shopping trips to Mexico or gaming trips to Laughlin, Nevada. This attractive off-the-road alternative during the winter months will fit nicely into the budget plan.

The monthly campground fees should be reasonable, fuel expenditures will drop to a few dollars a month, and the

Pool Complex at "The Meadows", Mission, Texas

inexpensive or free park activities will ease the recreational budget. It avoids the uncertainty of getting a camping site at a public park during the popular winter and holiday season. Strong friendships are formed at these winter parks and some return year after year to the same park. It's fun to watch the greetings and hugs as the regulars return. Yes, there are tears when the farewells are made in the early spring. The snow-birds will head north to catch up on work around the house, and their full-timing friends will head to places like the Grand Canyon, Yellowstone or who knows where.

Some full-timers are interested in the many specialty type commercial parks. We enjoyed our stay at a ranch near Ft Davis, Texas. The 2,000-acre ranch had a small full hookup RV park as a part of it's many other guest services. The weekly rate was affordable and the hospitality was genuine Texan. The ranch had an indoor heated swimming pool and a stable of riding horses. The highlight of our visit occurred when the manager asked us to assist the ranch hands in rounding up some horses that had been out to pasture for a couple of weeks. For an afternoon we played cowboy. What fun! There are many other ranches that have RV facilities as part of their operations.

Other commercial parks cater to those who like to square dance, golf, or fish. A campground may have a huge dance hall or be adjacent to a golf course; or it may have an ocean side marina with all the necessary services, or be situated on a river or lake.

For those liking roller coasters or theme parks, it's nice to know that many of them have RV parks as a part of their operations. Two that we have visited are Cedar Pointe at Sandusky, Ohio, and Disney World (Fort Wilderness) at Orlando, Florida. It was really handy when we could slip over to our RV for an afternoon nap or stay late at the park (less crowded) knowing that home was only a few steps away. These parks are expensive, but not compared to the hotel rooms in these areas. Besides most people can't take more than a couple days at an amusement park so the visit will be short.

When we first started full-timing, we didn't think that commercial parks would be important to our operational plan. We have since found that a public park is not always convenient and it isn't always cost effective traveling extra miles to stay at a membership park. Not only that, holiday times at membership parks are often reserved for home park members. There are also times when we don't wish to be moving every week and monthly rates in commercial parks are attractive. We have found that when used intelligently, and as part of an overall plan, commercial parks can be an asset and are another tool available to enhance the life of a full-timer.

♥ ♥

From Barb's Diary

Friday, March 31, 1989, We are at Hueston Woods State Park in Ohio. Here it is our first full day as full-timers and we woke up early to hear rain. We have a Cincinnati country radio station on, and the forecast is for rain all day. It will get down to 27 tonight. Sure hope we don't freeze up. Now at 7:30 in the morning, it is snowing. Honest! What a dirty trick. Guess we will just stay home today. Good thing that I brought my winter coat. It's really snowing hard, but it's not sticking.
Later, We took our gym bags and headed toward Hamilton. It looked like a good sized town, but there was no gym there. A lady in the drug store directed us to another part of town and a spa. Ron and I both worked out for two hours then ate lunch at Bob Evans. Came back and relaxed. The TV is a problem—where to put it. I hate it anyway. We turned it off and read. Went to bed at 10 p.m.
Saturday, April 1, 1989, Too cold. Never got the bikes off the car. It wasn't bad though. We kept warm inside.
Sunday, April 2, 1989, Went to church—nice service. Then just stayed in the motorhome—too cold and too rainy.
Monday, April 3, 1989, Left Hueston Woods—took the scenic route to General Butler State Park in Carrollton, Kentucky. It's warm and not raining. This is a nice park. We're all set up—tablecloth on the picnic table, lawn chairs out and bikes off. We rode the park including the big hill to the lodge. Buds are on the trees—walked a lot too. Nice to have water hookups. Took showers in here.
Wednesday, April 5, 1989, Left General Butler for the drive to Mammoth Cave. It was only a 150-mile drive. Cloudy day but pretty drive. Campground is nice and nearly empty. Some tenters which surprised us since it's so cold. Yukky damp cold! We got our mail right away. That works great. Also got tickets for the half day cave tour on Thursday.
Thursday, April 6, 1989, Since the sun was shinning in the a.m., we tried biking, but it was too cold so we hiked two

miles to the Green River—stiff walk. Then we did the cave tour which was four and one half hours of strenuous walking. Met a single deaf man who lives in his van most of the time. He has been doing this for five years. Told us to be sure to visit Yosemite National Park in California. Said we must spend at least a week there. He is a neat guy—a greatgrandfather. Said he cries every time he sees Yosemite. Will have to look it up on the map.

Friday, April 7, 1989, We're leaving—nearly froze last night. Without electricity, we couldn't run the furnace—battery is low. This is like tenting only more comfortable. Ron started the engine and we were able to run the furnace to warm us up a bit. The bed was warm and cozy. Guess we've got to go further south.

Wednesday, April 12, 1989, Old Stone Fort State Park, Tennessee. We're happy—got to hike about five miles around the old stone fort and along the Little and Big Duck rivers and their falls. It was quite a hike just to the museum and back too. It's not a real big park. There are only two other campers here. We are leaving right now for Fall Creek Falls State Park. It is only a 60-mile drive.

Later, What a scary ride. It was up and down one mountain after another—switchbacks and so scary from my side of the motorhome. Then when we got to the park, it was miles and miles of driving just to get to the campground. This park is huge. The biggest we have ever been in—lots of hiking and biking and everything.

Thursday, April 13, 1989, Last night we had a nice campfire after great hamburgs and beans. Then we played Yahtzee before bed—no TV—just music. This a.m. Ron is going to cook sausage and eggs outside then we will go biking to the lodge and falls. It's going to get up to 65 today. That's great.

Monday, April 17, 1989, We've been having so much fun here that I haven't had time to write. We have enjoyed exploring this beautiful park. There were two other motorhomes here when we came. They left and we were totally alone in this huge campground (100 sites). It was great—so quiet and beautiful. Days are warmer. Friday and Saturday nights there were a few more campers, but it was still quiet. We hiked and biked to Fall Creek Falls and Piney Falls. Wow! Saturday it was misty so we drove a big circle which included McMinn-ville and that Exxon Station with Jannie's Pies (yummy). We found a Kroger grocery store and stocked up on veggies. Ate lunch in a little restaurant on top of Spencer's Mountain. We each had a sandwich, coffee and pie. Whole thing cost $6.10. Everyone in the family works there.

Today we rode our bikes to Hwy 111 at the south entrance and back, then more in the park for a total of 25 miles. We've gotten our mail twice. It's a long drive to the post office in Pikeville since a bridge is out—30 miles each way. Every night we drive to the lodge to make the phone call to our service. Every night we see lots of deer by the road. We've been eating good and enjoying the good life. Oh, today the birds were serenading us. So many different kinds. It was great. The sounds of nature are wonderful!

From the March 1992 issue of Movin' On

WHAT A LIFE
A Tucson Luxury Resort

Over two years ago, we were hiking up to the top of Guadalupe Mountain in western Texas, and during a rest break stopped to talk to a hiker who was heading down the trail. In the short conversation that followed, he found out we were full-timers and that we were heading to Arizona. He enthusiastically suggested that we camp at the Voyager campground in Tucson. He gave us a little overview of the place, and I made a mental note to go there someday. I don't remember what specific things he said, but I did remember the name.

We didn't end up near Tucson that time or the next year either, but on our way to Texas from California, we made a special trip to check out this campground.

He was right. It is the absolute best place we have ever stayed. I mean if you are looking for level, landscaped, wide sites with good hookups and a million things to do, this is the place.

After Ron registered in the office, he returned to the motorhome and exclaimed that the office was like a hotel lobby. He went on to describe the three teller type windows in the plush lounge. An escort led us to our site and made sure we lined up properly (it was so easy—a pull through—and I didn't have to get out of the motorhome to help). Didn't have to use any boards to level either, so we were all set-up in no time.

When Ron registered he was given a newsletter of all that was going on the next two weeks. There were thirty some pages and each page—both sides—was crammed full of all that was available. Just the basic listing of each day's schedule took three pages.

The activities begin as early as 7 a.m. and go on until evening. Every hour on the hour and half hour there are at least one and as many as ten different activities happening at once. Here is the list for just one Monday; 7 a.m.—Yoga; 8 a.m. Yoga, Co-Ed exercises, Tennis (inter play), beginning stained glass; 9 a.m. beginning ceramics, aquacise, stenciling, bridge lessons, clogging (beginning), volleyball, shuffleboard (open play), silvercraft (open shop), Lapidary (open shop); 10 a.m. clogging (easy), camcorder lessons, Spanish, zipper sand art; 11 a.m. clogging (easy—intermediate), tennis (ladies doubles); NOON clogging (int); 1 p.m. square dancing workshop, computer class, shuffleboard (open play), Canasta, Nimblefingers, wood shop (open shop), stained glass, silvercraft (open shop), Lapidary (open shop), Oil painting, silvercraft; 3 p.m. Square dancers hoedown, volleyball; 6 p.m. clock class, silvercraft (beg), stained glass (open shop); 7 p.m. party bridge, poker, nickel bingo, woodshop training; 7:30 Square dancing. Add to this all the special breakfasts, dinners, concerts, programs and. . . LOTS going on.

There are over 1,000 full hookup sites and the daily rate was $20. We stayed 10 days and got the weekly rate of $122 for the week and our 10% Good Sam discount on the remaining days. Oh, it was worth it. The daily and weekly rates include electricity. Those who go for a month at a time must pay electricity but get a nice monthly rate of $369. The annual rate is $1,848, and again you must pay electricity. It gets cool in the evenings and hot in the summer so heaters and air conditioners are necessary.

This park is privately owned by local professional people and not financed. They have paid as they added and improved the park and they are still expanding. That is pretty important if you are thinking about long term parking. A number of park models (small mobile homes) are available, and many park residents have a home elsewhere (usually up north) but spend the entire winter at the Voyager. They have a huge lot for RV storage. Those who come for the winter to stay in their park model often drive an RV down—enjoying a leisurely drive and sightseeing then store the RV until time to go home. Again, going home is another adventure. What a life!!

The Voyager is so complete that one never needs to leave the park. They have a post office, restaurant, and convenience market. We tried all three. The market is well stocked, and the restaurant served delicious food. They both have specials all the time—just like "downtown."

As far as sports things, they have everything except a golf course (they do have a putting green and golf driving nets). Two pools, two jacuzzies, sauna, exercise room, volleyball, badminton and tennis courts, shuffleboard, horseshoes, basketball, miniature golf, croquet, table tennis and billiards complete the list. Add to that all the craft and game rooms plus the huge ballroom and you have quite a complex.

Every morning while there, we joined many others who go for their morning walks. We like to walk a 15 minute mile and were able to walk for one hour (4 miles) going up and down the rows of RVs and park models and never walked the same road twice.

We attended the non-denominational church service in the ballroom on Sunday morning. There were over 300 in attendance and the service was very enjoyable. Everyone arrives 30 minutes before the service starts for hymn singing. They have a talented organist plus a piano player, and their choir, which is 50 members strong, gave me goose bumps when they sang the anthem.

It just made my heart sing to see so many senior citizens enjoying life to the fullest. Everyone is so active, happy and young looking. We had fun. I finally got my fill of bridge for a while. If we were there for a month, I wouldn't play every day like we did.

Check out this place if you're in southern Arizona. It is just off I-10 at exit 270 (Kolb Road).

♥ ⌂ ♥

5

WHERE WILL WE LIVE?
Membership Campgrounds

In Chapter 4 we discussed an array of options available to full-timers through the use of public and private campgrounds. They are important in the overall operational plan for a full-timer. In our opinion, however, every full-timer will also want to consider a membership park or two in order to complete their wide range of camping options. Imagine being able to camp in luxurious campgrounds for free, or as little as one dollar a night, at over 500 locations around the United States, Canada and Mexico. These campgrounds will welcome you as family. Most of the membership campgrounds have full hook-up sites in a scenic setting, pools, saunas, and a club house with many activities. Out-of-state license plates dominate the campsites, and many belong to full-timers. Often the membership parks will have cabins or trailer units for rent at very reasonable rates too. They can be used by family members when they visit.

The key to benefiting from a membership park is usage, in order to write off the initial costs of membership and subsequent annual fees. It figures then, that full-timers could use and benefit from the membership system far more than others. Used repeatedly, the entire investment can be recouped in a short time. Later in this chapter, we will work out, on paper, the financial benefit of a membership park to a full-timer.

There are different types of private membership parks. All provide camping privileges for members, but the conditions, amenities and organizational affiliations vary widely. Some private parks convey deeded property while others may operate under a condominium type organizational structure. These later arrangements may meet a need for a nesting place and give a feeling of permanence that some full-timers desire. Obviously, this arrangement will allow longer stays. Most of the membership parks, however, only sell camping privileges and the amenities that go with memberships.

In order to attract memberships, the parks offer a wide range of amenities. Our own home park offers a large indoor swimming pool, saunas, jacuzzi, tennis courts, private lake with beach and fishing, restaurant, club house and many member activities. We have visited other parks that have golf courses and riding stables in addition to many of the above benefits. Membership in a park can be enhanced with affiliations of other parks in the network. Some of the best known national organizations are: Camp Coast to Coast (CCC), Thousand Trails (TT), National Association of Campground Owners (NACO), and Resort Parks International (RPI). A membership in a park affiliated with one or more of these organizations will allow use of member facilities across the country for a very modest fee. Usually, when camping at the home park, there is no fee. When camping within the network

Poolside at a Washington State CCC

system, rates are nominal and range from free to $1 a night. Maintenance fees charged to the park's own members provide operational funds. We pay annual membership fees to operate our park. Members affiliated with CCC visit our park and we visit theirs. A nice arrangement.

Membership costs, depending on the amenities and ownership rights, may run from $3,000 to $12,000. In addition, the annual maintenance fee may range between $100 and $500. The national campground affiliation membership fee will probably be in the $50-$100 range. A private membership park can be a considerable investment.

There is a secondary market for campground memberships that are available for transfer to another owner. While large discounts can be realized, the purchaser should investigate to assure that the membership resort is in good financial condition, and that the transfer is made properly. Another word of caution—the national affiliation membership does not transfer automatically, and the new owner must make application as a member in good standing of a member campground. The application is usually accepted; however, it's best to investigate.

The idea of camping for a $1 a night is very attractive to full-timers and the national affiliation becomes the primary reason for joining, although a nice home park near your former home or family can offer advantages. The concept of these membership parks is fairly new and like many new organizations there have been problems. Problems occur when the home park or home park chain is under-financed, under-sold, plagued with delinquent membership fees, or poorly managed. With proper investigation, an investment in a membership park can bring great dividends to a full-timer. If you are primarily interested in the network affiliation, and a home park is not important, the secondary market could be very cost effective. A typical secondary membership can be purchased in the $1500-$2000 range. Even if there is an element of risk, it doesn't take long for a full-timer to recoup that cost when saving the $12 to $30 a night charged by commercial campgrounds. Secondary memberships are advertised in RV magazines such as *Trailer Life*, *Motorhome*, Good Sam's *Highways* , and *Family Motor Coaching*. They may be purchased directly from individuals or companies that specialize in this market. Thousand Trails is now offering resales direct from the company. Other full-timers and RVers can be helpful in identifying sound, well-run home parks.

Some parks have very low annual maintenance fees while others have frozen maintenance fees. This feature may be helpful in selling memberships, but it can affect the financial stability of a park. Most of the initial membership fee goes for selling expenses and investment in the park's infrastructure. Therefore, it is important to a park's financial health to have a reasonable maintenance fee and to be able to raise that fee when costs go up.

Our home park has a maintenance fee that cannot be raised beyond a national cost of living index. State laws and national campground organizations generally place a restriction on the number of times a campsite can be sold, which is usually ten times. Therefore, a sold out park with two hundred sites and an annual maintenance fee of $200, will have an annual maintenance income of $400,000. Depending on the amenities, this should be enough to maintain the park. If fees are frozen and maintenance costs rise, the park will suffer. We have seen this happen. When things fall apart, it is usually down hill from there. As a full-timer you may not be interested in the amenities at the home park, but they make it easier for the park to sell memberships. That makes the membership more valuable.

In many cases the original investment can be recouped in less than a year. Our method of evaluating a membership is conservative and what you would expect from a retired accountant. Multiply the membership investment by 8% (or whatever the current savings rate is), add the annual membership fees (home park maintenance fee and national affiliation) and divide by the cost of spending a night in a campground minus the membership nightly charge, if there is one. In figuring the actual cost, it is necessary to calculate the earnings on the membership investment as if that amount were left in savings. Assuming a commercial campground full-hookup cost of $12 a night (low), this figure will show the number of nights needed to camp for $1 a night (CCC) in order to break even on the investment. For example:

Campground Membership Cost ($4,000 x 8%)	$320.00
Home Park Annual Maintenance Fees	200.00
National Affiliation Dues	50.00
Total Annual Cost	$ 570.00

$570 divided by $11 ($12 less $1) is approximately 52.

Therefore, given the above costs, it will be necessary to camp at membership parks 52 times during the year to break even on an investment of $4000 and annual fees of $250. As full-timers, we plan to use our CCC membership at least half of the time or 180 days a year. Even though our costs are slightly higher than the example, we benefit financially from the membership. Apply our usage to the above example and the return on a $4,000 investment would be considerable. 180 days minus the 52 to break even computes to 128 free days of camping. Multiply 128 days by the $11 used above and it results in an investment return of $1408 in addition to the 8%. At that rate the original $4000 will be recouped in less than three years, while earning a good rate of interest.

More importantly, we could never get into a park for just $12 and enjoy all of the amenities of the Camp Coast to Coast system. This would also be true of the other national membership park networks. Like public and commercial campgrounds, membership parks can be another tool in the full-timing adventure.

1994 editor's note: As of 1994, Coast to Coast has allowed parks to designate four months out of the year as their peak season. These are marked in the directory and are not necessarily consecutive months. During each park's peak season visiting Coast to Coasters must pay an additional $3 per night. As far as we are concerned, it is still a bargain.

♥   ♥

From the September 1991 issue of Movin' On

COAST TO COAST UPDATE

by Ron

Many of our readers are members of the Coast to Coast Campground network. Those of you that are, know that CCC members often exchange information about the CC campgrounds that they visit.

We thought that a monthly column commenting briefly on our CC campground experience would be helpful to you. Those of you who are not members may also be interested. So.......here goes for this month.

Coarsegold, California, (Yosemite South) pg 64 Beautiful setting, convenient to Yosemite and Fresno, friendly staff, good sites, nice pool. They regularly serve great breakfasts at a reasonable price.

Isleton, California, (Delta Isle) pg 77 Good location, near Napa Valley and San Francisco, great for boating, cycling, fishing. Lots of full hookups, easy to get in. Sites are narrow and maintenance is poor.

Klamath, California, (Klamath River RV Park) pg 81 Great location in the middle of Redwood National Park. Very friendly. Good hookups, sites are narrow, on the river, very scenic.

Talent, Oregon, (Oregon RV Roundup) pg 385 Lovely park, well maintained, good swimming pool, nice sites, park is next to a bike path. Limited sites for large rigs; reservations suggested. Tons of blackberry bushes along the bike path. Seven miles from Ashland and the famous Shakespearean theaters.

La Pine, Oregon, (Land of Lakes Resort) pg 379 Easy to get in, lots of wide full hookup sites. This is a friendly, very basic park about 25 miles south of Bend. No trees, no pool, nice club house.

Bend, Oregon, (Sundance Meadows) pg 377 Water and electric only, poor interior roads and narrow—sloping sites. This 900 acre ranch offers horseback riding. It also has an indoor pool which is very nice, but it's a half mile from the camp sites on a very rough road.

From the October 1991 issue of Movin' On

COAST TO COAST UPDATE

by Ron

We continue to enjoy our Coast to Coast membership and would like to share our CCC experiences with you in this monthly column. This month all of our experiences were good—several being outstanding.

Mosier, Oregon, (American Adventure—Columbia River Gorge) pg 381. This resort was voted most scenic of all CCC resorts by it's members. It's true. It's worth the long 1,200 foot climb and 1-½ mile of gravel road to get here. The amenities include a nice pool, hot tub and par three golf course. Sites are secluded and wooded with water and electricity only. Big rigs may have difficulty maneuvering into sites.

Silver Creek, Washington, (Leisure Time Resorts—Paradise) pg 487. This is truly a five star luxury resort. It has everything including sundaes every day at 3 o'clock. Sites are wide and wooded with most being pull-throughs. The swimming complex will rival the Ritz.

Snoqualmie, Washington, (Leisure Time Resorts—Cascade) pg 488. Very similar to its sister resort above. Only difference is that the hookups include only water and electricity. Many of the sites are pull-throughs. Location is great— very handy to Seattle.

Soap Lake, Washington, (American Adventure—Soap Lake Resort "Healing Waters") pg 489. Good hookups and roomy sites including pull-throughs. Nice pool, but facilities were in need of maintenance— like many American Adventure resorts, this one is experiencing financial problems.

Polson, Montana, (Flathead Lake) pg 285. Great location with well maintained pool, rest rooms, hot tub and club house. Sites are narrow and could be soggy at certain times of the year. Right on the lake, it would be a great place in the summer.

Anaconda, Montana, (Fairmont) pg 284. Hookups are awkward and we needed to use our 75-foot hose. Next door to a complete conference complex also owned by the resort. There is a small charge to use.

From The December 1992 Issue Of Movin' On

COFFEE BREAK

Take a break. Get a cup of coffee and let's chat.

I have a problem understanding the financial feasibility of membership camp- grounds...in your book, you state..."a 200 site park with an annual maintenance fee of $200 will have a maintenance income of $400,000." My arithmetic comes up with $40,000.
Mary Lee Page, Huntsville, AL

Your concern about Coast to Coast memberships brings back memories. We too were very con- cerned and put off joining the CCC system for almost two years. Now we wonder what we were worried about. Except for one time, we have always been treated like old friends, when we arrive at a CC Campground.

Are you familiar with time shares? If you bought a time share instead of a condo, you could only use it certain times of the year, and you aren't the only owner—in fact you own nothing—only the right to stay there once a year (or some-

thing like that). The CCC system works like that. When you buy into a CC Camp- ground, you are buy- ing the privilege to camp there. Again you do not own an inch of property. Ron mentioned the 200 site park. They don't just sell to 200 people. They can sell 10 memberships for each site or a total of 2,000 (for that 200 site park). Now do you see where we came up with that $400,000 maintenance income (2,000 X $200)?

You can visit some CC Camp- grounds by purchasing coupons of- fered in the RV magazines by CCC. The coupons sell for $59.95 and are good for six nights of camping. Ten dollars a night is not a bad price for camping and you will not get a sales pitch. After you decide on a campground, then watch the ads for a secondary membership. It's not a bad risk because if you spend six months a year camping, it wouldn't take long to recoup your original investment. The best deal is to buy a member- ship on the secondary market. You will find ads for these parks in *FMCA, Motorhome, Highways*, and *Trailer Life* magazines. These parks are still legitimate parks, and if you were to buy a new membership you would pay several thousand dollars. But someone wants out—perhaps a spouse died or the couple doesn't want to camp anymore. You really can get a good deal this way. We have friends who just bought into a park near Branson, Missouri, for only $800. They checked out the park first (by visiting it) and talked to the members who were camping there. That is the only way to check out a park since they are privately owned. Gut feeling counts too. Look around and see if things are being taken care of.

Another comforting thing is that if your park does go broke, Coast to Coast will usually assign you "orphan" status, and you will be picked up by another park for a nominal amount or just the annual maintenance fee. For that reason, some buy the cheapest membership they can buy and just wing it.

On the road, you may stay at each of the 500 CCC parks for two weeks each year. Each week must be separated by a month out of the park. This is great for traveling, and in many areas, like Houston, Texas, there are seven CCCs within a 50 mile radius. We can go to one, stay a week, go to another, stay a week, and so on. By the time we have stayed one week at each of the seven parks, we could do the

whole thing over again starting at the first park where we originally stayed. The month would be over. Using this example, we could camp for 14 weeks for only $98 (14 X 7 X $1).

So you wonder how they can make it at $1 per night. That is not where they get their money. The money to "make it" comes from the membership's annual maintenance fees. The dollar is just a token; probably because if it was totally free, it wouldn't mean as much. The CC benefits are just part of the selling feature when the home membership is purchased. It really works out to be a nice trade in most cases. You buy a membership in your park and I buy one in mine. I could stay at mine for free and you could stay at yours for free, but we're going to trade for a week. You come to my park and I'll go to yours. That's all it is.

Most CC parks do not take in regular campers off the road. But we have been running across more that do, and that concerns us. It is usually in the heavy tourist areas. We recently stayed at the CCC park in Lakeland and noticed that they take regular campers off the road at $19 per night (off season rate). It was no problem in November; but, unless you like crowds, don't go to Florida or Arizona from January thru March, and you won't have these problems. That is only sensible.

♥ ⬦ ♥

6

WHERE WILL WE LIVE?

Saving Money And Having Fun

There's no question that campground fees represent a major part of the full-timer's budget. This chapter will offer ideas on how to reduce that to almost nothing and in some cases add to the full-timer's income. Not only have full-timers found ways to reduce or eliminate camping costs, they have a lot of fun doing it. There are three principle ways of camping free.

1. Dry camping in a "no charge" area, either public or private (boondocking).
2. Volunteering in public campgrounds.
3. Assisting in commercial campgrounds.

Boondocking

Boondocking takes many different forms and approaches. Overnight boondocking is common among full-timers. It's done as much for convenience as it is to save money. When in route to a new location overnight campgrounds may be out of the way, full, or too expensive. That is when full-timers often seek out a well traveled highway rest area, a well lighted church parking lot, or a shopping center parking lot. Some prefer an out-of-the-way school yard, country road or an abandoned business parking lot; however, from a safety standpoint, we prefer to be where there are other people. Before full-timing, we were in a hurry to get to Maryland and were traveling the Pennsylvania turnpike late at night. Becoming sleepy, we nestled in between two large trucks at a rest area for five or six hours sleep and felt perfectly safe.

Extended stay boondocking, however, is another matter and takes some planning and ingenuity. Our experience in long term dry camping is very limited, and we can only relate what we have heard from other full-timers who swear by it.

Southern climate boondocking at well known boondocking sites is popular among many full-timers and snowbirds on a limited income. Some do it just for the camaraderie of fellow campers, and they seem to love it. The Arizona desert town of Quartzite is a popular spot for winter boondockers. Thousands flock there for free camping, sunshine, companionship, rock hounding, and a gigantic ongoing flea market. Hundreds of others camp free all winter along the beaches on North Padre Island in Texas, and we have heard of Corps of Engineer parks in southern Florida that are popular for boondocking.

All of these areas have nearby dump station facilities, but dry camping is the order of the day. Full-timers who boondock as a way of life are very adept at it. Solar panels, generators, invertors, homemade solar water heaters, extra propane bottles, campfires, sponge baths, careful water usage, and warm comforters are a part of their everyday life. The selection of an RV is important when considering boondocking as part of the full-timing plan. Insulation, holding tank capacity, fresh water tank, generator, propane tanks, and solar panels become important.

Boondocking, like membership parks, can be another tool in the new life of full-timing. Those who contemplate doing a lot of boondocking will want to invest in several books that list free camping spots. One such book is *Guide To Free Campgrounds* by Don Wright and is available through Cottage Publications, 24396 Pleasant View Drive, Elkhart, IN 46517. The price of the book is $13.95.

Volunteering At Public Parks

Volunteering at public parks, national monuments or historical sites takes many forms. Most volunteer assignments offer the availability of a free spot to park, usually with hookups. However, those who volunteer agree that the biggest benefit is the satisfaction of contributing to our country's park system while meeting many wonderful people. Many full-timers find that a combination of boondocking and volunteering actually takes care of their campground costs with little or no expenditure. Unlike some of us, they don't feel the need for a campground membership.

A common type of public volunteering is campground hosting. A campground host is the eyes and ears of the ranger staff and is there to help campers with park information, rule interpretation, campsite selection, and with emergencies requiring outside assistance. Generally, campground hosts will help the ranger with camper registration recording those who have not registered. Campground hosts may also assist in litter pickup, but it usually is not mandatory. Likewise, most hosts are not required to clean rest rooms. The work is not hard, the hours are usually short, and many full-timers like

Our Free Campsite At Yosemite

the opportunity to meet and help people. If there is a negative to campground hosting, it relates to rule interpretation and turning people away from full campgrounds. Although not expected to enforce park regulations, rangers expect hosts to deal with minor infractions, and it may be your job to ask people to quiet down, turn off a generator after hours, control a camp fire or deal with other minor violations. In the case of repeated or serious violations, you are expected to contact a ranger via a radio that is provided.

Some prefer camp hosting in remote areas; however, they may not have hookups. There is a spot in Michigan's Upper Peninsula (Pictured Rocks National Lakeshore) where the National Park Service provides a generator, gasoline and radio to the campground hosts. The hosts pump their own water and are lucky to see a ranger once a month. The hosts, that we talked to, loved the serene campground right on the shores of Lake Superior. We have found that many couples are well suited to campground hosting, while others are not.

Although we have done some campground hosting, our favorite volunteer assignments have to do with park

Barb & Ron At "Work" In Yosemite

interpretation. We love to work at visitor centers where we provide information, lead walks, act as resource people, and even give bus tours. We remember, with fondness, a two month period in Yosemite National Park, California, when we were "pioneers" in the Pioneer Yosemite History Center. Dressed as early 20th century pioneers, we played the part of Wells Fargo agents assigned to Yosemite Park in 1915. There we could meet and visit with people while providing a living interpretation of the early history of Yosemite National Park.

Other great volunteer assignments we have had were Hot Springs National Park at Hot Springs, Arkansas, and the Lyndon B. Johnson National Historic Park at Stonewall, Texas. At the LBJ Park, our campsite was right on the LBJ ranch under some beautiful live oak trees. Visitor center work is as varied as the talents of the volunteer, and the parks appreciate all help. At Big Bend National Park we met a

Granddaughter Liisa At Work

geologist who was volunteering his services, and at Hot Springs National Park, volunteer Loren was the "Jack of all trades"—handy man. On the backpacking trail at Pictured Rocks, we met a volunteer backpacker whose job it was to hike from one end of the park to the other and back again checking on the conditions of the trail and assisting hikers. Computer experts, ecologists, ranch hands, whatever your talent, you'll be welcome.

At Hot Springs we conducted thermal feature tours, worked on the visitor desk, in the book store, and did a little computer work. At the LBJ National Historic Park, we both drove and narrated bus tours of the LBJ ranch which included President Johnson's first school, his birthplace, his final resting place, "Texas White House," and the ranch with all the beautiful Hereford cattle. Occasionally we worked at President Johnson's birthplace and gave short talks to the visitors.

Volunteer work in parks need not be limited to national

parks. Many state and local parks have a volunteer program. The Army Corps of Engineers also uses volunteers in their parks. Public budgets are always being squeezed, and recreational budgets are usually the first to be cut. Public officials will be the first to tell you that they could not operate the parks as well without the many volunteers on which they depend. Truly, there are a lot of volunteer positions available.

Our Home At The LBJ Ranch

A letter or telephone call to the area of your choice will get you on the right path to an application. The National Park Service has a standard application form that can be mailed to the Superintendent (Attention: VIP Coordinator) of the park selected. VIP stands for Volunteers In Parks. We have found that a phone call will often get the application rolling because the understaffed rangers are busy and often wait until the last minute before arranging for volunteers. Ask to speak to the VIP coordinator.

When starting out, it may be best to begin in a small park to gain experience and become acquainted with park personnel. After awhile, volunteers become known in the park system as rangers transfer to other locations. They often suggest that volunteers come and work for them at their new assignment. This happened to us at Hot Springs National Park. One of the rangers was transferred to Yosemite and the next summer we joined him there.

Some of the well-known parks have more applications than they need and often have yearly returnees. Do not despair—there are more than enough volunteer positions to go around. Since there is some training involved and arrangements have to be made, many parks set a minimum volunteer period of 60 or 90 days. If you are prepared to stay longer, they will love you for it.

A real benefit to volunteering is that we are in one place for two to three months and get to know the area well. The parks are usually scenic with many hiking trails or roads to explore, and nearby towns are fun to visit. Volunteering can be economical. We find that besides using little money for gasoline, we save by getting to know the local grocery stores and shop the specials. Since we are not brand new to the area, we don't feel the need to eat out as often as when we are traveling.

Volunteering also forces us to learn more than we ever thought we could know about an area. As interpreters, we need to research our subject in order to talk about it. Probably the best reason to volunteer is to meet all the wonderful rangers along with the people who visit the park. Our work is appreciated by both, and it is nice to feel that we are helping to make a park visit enjoyable.

A final word about volunteer positions in parks: depending on budget constraints, some parks offer a small per diem to their volunteers. This varies even within the National Park system where some parks can offer a small stipend while others can barely afford to provide an identification badge. Some offer uniforms and others can't even spare a cap. When campground hosting, some park rangers are good about providing firewood and propane while others neglect this necessity. Conveniences, perks, and hours should be thoroughly discussed before agreeing to provide free labor. Consider the remoteness of the park and the local prices. It could turn out to be a budget disaster (in spite of free camping) if it's necessary to travel miles for groceries or propane while paying exorbitant tourist prices.

Assisting In Commercial Campgrounds

A great marriage of convenience is often entered into between full-timers and owners of commercial campgrounds. They both need what the other party has. The full-timer needs a place with hookups, a few dollars spending money and something to do in order to keep busy (but not too much). The campground owner cannot afford to pay high wages for help, needs experienced mature help and usually has extra spaces or can create one. Couples often work as a team with the husband doing routine maintenance work and the wife working in the office or camp store. Hours and duties can be negotiated along with salary. If duties are minimal, the arrangement may be just for the camping spot with propane thrown in. Some campgrounds also offer discounts on groceries and supplies.

We once visited a commercial campground in the Smoky Mountain area that employed over a dozen couples as camp hosts. At this large campground, each couple put in 20 hours each (40 total) performing easy tasks. Those tasks included checking gate passes, selling snacks at the pool, driving a minibus to tourist spots, picking up litter and visiting with guests. There existed a camaraderie among the couples. They were enjoying their work, each others company, and had pot-lucks among themselves several times a week. Their pay was a home for the summer, propane, firewood and lots of fun times.

Advertisements for campground helpers can be found in most RV periodicals and in *Workamper News*, a bimonthly paper that lists both volunteer and paying campground jobs.

Workamper News advertisers target full-timers. For a free brochure, call *Workamper News at 1-800-446-5627 or write to them at 201 Hiram Rd, Heber Springs, AR, 72543.* Many federal and state parks also advertise in Workamper News.

Full-timer friends of ours, Liz and Cal Mc Gee, spent a summer in the Adirondack Mountains at a beautiful campground. They loved the work and the owners gave them full reign of the campground with a lot of perks. The next summer they worked as campground hosts at another private park in Estes Park, Colorado. And most recently they were found working at a campground in Oregon.

While at 29 Palms, California, the owners of a new campground offered us the opportunity to stay and help them straighten out their office. They had built a beautiful campground with their own labor—complete with all the amenities, but were having trouble with the administrative part of running the campground. They offered a lovely spot free if we would stay and help them a few hours a week. We were really tempted because that type of work is right up our alley, but we had already made commitments to be volunteers at the LBJ National Historic Park in Texas and had to move on.

By now it should be obvious that it is not difficult to exchange a little labor or service for a campground spot. It can be fun and very cost effective. At the very least, campground fees can be eliminated from the budget for a few months, and nothing is forever.

♥   ♥

The Following Are Two Articles From The July 1991 Issue of Movin' On. The Setting is Yosemite National Park in Northern California

LIVING HISTORY
Fun For Everyone

The Pioneer Yosemite History Center (PYHC) in Wawona officially opened on Wednesday, June 23 after a week of intense preparation. History had to be researched and learned so the players could portray real people from Yosemite's past. This is living history.

Except for the covered bridge and the grey barn, all of the buildings in the center were moved from their original locations. This collection of buildings represents different years in the evolution of the park and more importantly the people who lived, worked and made a contribution to Yosemite.

Just before crossing the covered bridge to actually enter the PYHC there is a big grey barn originally owned by the Washburns who also owned the nearby Wawona Hotel. Wawona was the largest stage stop in Yosemite in the late 1800's. Today, as in the past, the barn is used to harness and repair the stage. Now it is also used for the Saturday night barn dances.

The structure that literally bridges 1991 to the past is, in fact, the covered bridge. Nearly lost in a 1955 flood, its restoration was the first step in preserving the other buildings. Originally built as an uncovered bridge by Galen Clark in 1857, it was used by all Yosemite bound traffic. Clark had built a way station for visitors in Wawona. Later he sold his station and land along the river to the Washburns who were from Vermont, and they covered the bridge.

As one walks across the bridge, hearing the rush of the river underneath, other sounds come in to play. Chickens cackling, a rooster crowing, a hammer hitting iron at the blacksmith shop, and the clomp of the horse's hooves as they pull the stage, bring one back in time.

Visitors from all over the world are greeted by either Barb Hofmeister or Julie Schuller at the first cabin after the bridge. Barb or Julie is dressed in 1915's fashion complete with black high top shoes, black stockings, long skirt and long sleeved, high neck blouse while the tourists wear shorts and carry cameras and camcorders. The visitors are asked to stop for a few minutes and listen to a short orientation before going on. They are informed that the PYHC is not a village, that the buildings came from all over what is now Yosemite National Park, and the people who lived and worked in them did not know one another. "How would you like to actually go back in time," the hostess asks. Barbara continues:

"We'd like for you to pretend that when you enter each building, you are in the original location and in another time as well. For example, here at the artist studio it is 1900 and we are in Yosemite Valley, not Wawona. This is the studio of Christian Jorgenson. No one lived here, but lots of artists worked here; and if you had entered this building in 1900 it is very likely that it would be empty of people just as it is today. On such a nice day as this the artists would be out painting. I hope that this empty building will remind you that a building without people isn't very exciting. It is people that bring them to life. There are real people living and working in the rest of the buildings, and you get to meet them because you **will** be going back in time. Is anyone afraid of time travel?"

"The next cabin is the home of George Anderson. When you walk in the door it will be 1881. In case you have never heard of George, he is the first person to have climbed Half Dome, and, in fact, built the trail that is still used today. Now, perhaps, you'd like to know how he did that or how he lives, why he prefers a dirt floor to a wood floor, how he happened to come to Yosemite from Scotland—anything at all that you want to know about him—just ask him. Now is your chance to find out first hand. By the way, George intends to build a hotel on top of Half Dome. I think you'll agree that that would be quite a feat. Go ahead and ask him how he expects to accomplish that or why?"

"Next, you will go to the Hodgdon cabin and be back to 1889. Lots of good aromas come from this cabin because she is always baking cookies or bread. Mary Kay Hodgdon (a homesteader who came to California from Vermont in a covered wagon) and one or two of her grandchildren will be there. Now is your opportunity to ask all those questions you have always wanted to ask of a homesteader. Perhaps you don't remember your history and forgot what one had to do to homestead; or you'd like to know what that trip across the United States was like. Better yet, ask her what she thinks of the National Park idea because 1889 is just one year before Yosemite is to become a national park, and her family is going to lose their land. But maybe you'd rather know how often they take baths, where the children go to school, or what kind of toys they have, and what kind of chores they have to do."

"From there you can visit the blacksmith shop. The time will be

1900, and many visitors are coming into the park. Glen, the smithy, has a lot of work to do. He repairs stages, household items and shoes horses. Ask him about his job. How much does he get paid? How many hours does he work? Where is he from? Oh, and he does have some of his fancy iron work for sale at 1991 prices."

"The Cavalry office is the next stop in your time travel, and when you enter that building it will be 1905. You will meet Captain Devine and be able to ask him anything you want to know about the Cavalry's job in the park. From 1890, when Yosemite became a national park, until 1914, when they needed to prepare for World War I, 150 men from the Presido of San Francisco protected Yosemite. Their primary goals were to keep sheep, cattle, prospectors, poachers and lumberman out. You might want to ask him just how they managed all that and what their life was like here."

"When the Cavalry pulled out in 1914 there were only 15 civilian rangers to take their places. The National Park Service was not created until August of 1916. These civilian rangers had an even greater responsibility than the Cavalry because the automobile was allowed to enter the park in 1914, and they had to collect the fee to enter. When you go into the ranger patrol cabin, it will be 1915, and you will meet one of the rangers wives (the rangers are all out on patrol). Again you will have the opportunity to ask about their life and work in Yosemite at that time. Pretend you have just entered the park in your automobile and see what all is required of you. The fee in 1915 was $5, the same as it is today. If you think that it is outrageous, tell her so and have her explain why the fee is so high. Is their life here a lonely one? What do they do for entertainment? What are their wages? These are just some of the questions you might ask."

"The Degnan Bakery was originally connected to the Degnan's home in Yosemite Valley. Bridget started baking just a few loaves of bread, and now in 1915, at the height of the tourist season, will bake as many as 400 loaves a day in her remarkable oven. Be sure you look inside. In just a few minutes you will know that she is from Ireland. You might be interested in why she left Ireland and choose this part of California, how many children she has, and what their life is like in the Valley."

"The last stop on your time travel is the Yosemite Transportation Co. and Wells Fargo & Co. Express. Again, the time will be 1915, and you will be in Yosemite Valley. George and Nona Faber are the first agents to work and live in this new building. Their two room apartment is behind the offices. It is a very modern building with electricity, and telephone, and they no longer use horse drawn stages. Just last year (1914) they sold the last of the horse equipment when they purchased their second auto stage. Their stage runs from El Portal to the Valley and back, but if you want to go to Wawona they can sell you a ticket and have the Wawona Stage and Turnpike Company pick you up. That company is still using horse drawn stages, but it will be the last year for they too will completely switch to auto stages in 1916. You might want to ask them why they came here from Pennsylvania, what business they conduct from this building, how much it costs to stay in the Sentinel Hotel or make pretend arrangements to travel out of the park. Ask about what is going on in the world too—a war is brewing in Europe."

"We hope you enjoy your visit with us here in the Pioneer Yosemite History Center and remember to ask lots of questions—that is—except for 1991 questions. You see they haven't been there yet, and they simply won't know the answers. If you have any 1991 questions please come back and ask either Julie or myself. Oh, and one other thing. If some of the pioneers ask you why you are wearing your night clothes or underwear please do not be offended. You do see that you are just not properly dressed for these times."

From this introduction, the visitors go visiting at their own pace. Most of the actors in the PYHC are volunteers. All had to learn as much as possible about their cabin times in order to answer the many questions which range from "Who

is the president of the United States?" to "How is the electricity generated?" Some had to learn how to operate equipment. Ron, who plays the part of George Faber (Wells Fargo agent, telegraph operator, etc.) was supposed to learn the principles of the telegraph, how to repair telephone lines, fix telephones, and operate the letter press so when visitors asked how they work, he could portray the man effectively. Pat had to learn the complexities of the oven in her bakery, John had to learn the Cavalry equipment, and Mike had to learn how the cables were attached to Half Dome and how to make cedar shakes. Everyone had something complex to learn. Occasionally someone will ask a question that the actors do not know, but they do a remarkable job of covering up with a quick ad lib. And everyone is constantly learning.

Ron has had a unique situation here. He has two wives. Julie and Barbara take turns working as Nona in the stage office. Each also works half a day as hostess. He says that's why he hasn't learned about the telegraph yet. "Two women keep him too busy," he says. Truth is he wastes a lot of time arguing with the stage driver—part of the act.

All of the PYHC staff agree that it's most fun when the visitors ask good questions and really play along. It is a painless way to learn a little bit of history. And the visitors aren't the only ones learning.

MY VISIT TO YOSEMITE

by liisa paunonen

How many kids could live two weeks without TV or radio and be happy just listening to the birds and watching deer and coyote here in Yosemite National Park? Well I am and really enjoying myself.

I flew from West Palm Beach, Florida, to Fresno, California, on June 18, 1991, and my grandparents picked me up at the airport. Then we drove an hour and a half to get to the park where they have their motor home parked.

Besides studying our parts for the Pioneer History Center, we took a hike to see the big Sequoia trees (the largest living things on earth). Boy are they ever! We also hiked 11 miles to the Chilnualana Falls and back down. What a hike! The waters were so rough there. Two people died there last month because of the big rocks and fast waters. Some people just get too close and slip, but they are the stupid people.

Then, on Sunday, June 23, we had dress rehearsal. It was fun!!! I could hardly wait till that next Wednesday when we would really start work everyday.

We also had campfires every night, but some nights we just sat and played games. I saw lots of deer. They come right to you and even in your campsite. I also saw some coyotes. They just walked right by our camp site.

I think I better tell you more about my part in the Pioneer History Center and what it is. Well you can read my grandma's article to see what it is about, but I'll tell you about my part in it.

The time for my cabin is 1889. I am eight-year-old Minnie Hodgdon. My father, Tom, is a cattle rancher and a stage coach driver. As a driver, he never made one mistake. He is famous around here. But we have some bad news. Mr. Muir wants to take our 160 acres (homestead) away from us and make it a preserve, and if they take it away then we won't have land to graze our cattle.

I love my job here and I have met so many interesting people that come into my cabin. They were all interested in talking to me. I also want to thank all the people I worked with, like Mike. He's real great as George Anderson, and I learned most of my ways from him. Then Barbara—she is playing the part of my grandmother Mary Kay Hodgdon. I love to have her around. Then there is Julie who is a really fun person and Glen (he is the blacksmith). He helps eat all the goodies my grandmother and I bake in our cabin. John tells the silliest jokes. David is another one who likes to help out and eat all the goodies. I won't forget Pat, Jason and Rebecca in the bakery. I always enjoyed visiting them. I liked coming around to the ranger cabin and saying, "hi," to Jean and Marie. Marshall let me feed the horses carrots, and I liked riding the stage. Then, of course, I always enjoy visiting my grandparents in the Wells Fargo Office. But then there is Paul. He is nice and really is great at telling stories and making people understand things. But the ones I really want to thank most of all are my mother and father for sending me to Yosemite. I really had a great visit.

From The April 1993 Issue Of Movin' On

Yes, It's Serene Here

BUT WE'RE NOT ON VACATION

The LBJ National Historic Park ranch unit is in the little community of Stonewall, Texas. Situated in the center of the beautiful Hill Country of Texas — the gently rolling hills make for glorious vistas.

We wake up in the morning to the cheerful sound of birds and the cattle are often grazing just outside our fence. We are about four miles from state route 290 on a narrow ranch road which winds its way up and through the ranch. It is very quiet here—except for the songs of many different birds, the rustling of the leaves on the live oak tree under which we sit or the occasional mooing of the cattle. This is the highest part of the LBJ ranch—the part that LBJ loved the best. We can see the whole valley all around us and we feel honored to be able to set here for the three months that we volunteer.

When we returned this year, we felt like we were returning home. I guess sitting still for three months —the longest we have stayed in one spot since we started full-timing—could do that to you. We didn't have to prepare for our jobs this year—it was still there in our heads and just needed a quick refresher which only took a day.

Our work week (four days) starts on Wednesday. We try to get up at 6:00 a.m. if it is not raining. I put the coffee on, turn on the hot water heater and we dress for our walk. We are usually out the door by 6:15 and after a little stretching, are on our way. The day is just breaking and the air is fresh. There are many roads we can walk here. Part of the fun is deciding where to walk. In any direction, it is easy to walk 1 ½ to 2 miles. We see cattle, antelope and sheep on our way. Our walk is anywhere from three to four miles in length and gets us back to our house by 7:00 or a little after. The coffee is ready, we turn on Good Morning America for a few minutes to rest before getting ready for work.

When we are scheduled to drive busses, we need to be at the bus barn (a 5 minute walk from home) by 9:15. Ron likes to drive into Stonewall (4 ½ miles each way) first to get a newspaper and check on mail. Each bus driver has to check out his/her bus—start the engine, check such things as the tires, turn signals, radio, doors, microphone, tape player and so on.

The check-out takes about 15 minutes and the drive to the visitor center takes 15 minutes or so (the busses don't go very fast).

Now that it is the busy time here, they run four or five busses each day. The first always leaves the visitor center at 10:00 a.m. and the last leaves at 4:00 p.m. In between, the tour coordinator sends out the busses as the traffic bears. We have seen busses go out every 15 minutes and at other times only every 1 ½ hours. Bus 1 (usually a ranger) needs to be down at the visitor center by 9:45.

Once you find out what time your first run is, you pull the bus up to the loading area, help load the bus, chit chat with the visitors a few minutes, make safety announcements and take off. The 10 mile tour takes 1-1/2 hours. It starts at the state park, travels Ranch Road #1 for a mile, crosses the Pedernales River, enters the National Park and stops briefly at the Junction school where LBJ started school at the age of four. The next stop is the LBJ birthplace where the visitors get off the bus to tour the home. After touring the home, the passengers pay their respects at the Johnson family cemetery where LBJ is buried then continue the tour of the ranch which includes the grandparents farmhouse, the ranch house (the former Texas White House) and the ranch proper with all the cattle etc.

All the while we are driving the bus, we are imparting information to the 59 passengers—details of Johnson's early childhood, political years and retirement. Our goal is to help people better understand the 36th president of the United States.

After each run, we find out when our next tour will be. Often it is so busy that we just unload one bus, pull up to the loading area and take off again without a break. We do get somewhat of a break while the visitors are touring the birth place though.

We have done as many as four tours in one day, but usually only do two or three. If we are the last bus, we don't get home till near 6:00 p.m. Those of you who are still working know how fast an evening goes—what with fixing dinner and so on. No time for adventure. We do enjoy our visits with our volunteer neighbors in the evenings.

When we work at the birth place, we need to be there (2-½ miles away) by 9:00 a.m. After opening up the house and barn, putting up the flag, wheeling a wheelchair to the gate and so on, it is nearly time for the first bus to pull up. When the visitors arrive at the front of the house, we give them a short five minute introduction, then show them through the house. It takes about 20 minutes for each group to get through the house and grounds. In busy times, when busses are running every 15 minutes or every one-half hour, you can imagine there is not much chance to rest at that job. The last tour arrives at the house at about 4:20 p.m. and by the time they are gone and the house is closed up, it is usually 5:00 p.m. before we leave.

Ron and I both like driving the buses best. Being with a group for the 1-½ hour tour allows us to get to know the group a little better. So far this year Ron and I have conducted 119 tours.

We are off Sunday, Monday and Tuesday. Sunday is busy with church, laundry and grocery shopping. We usually don't get home from Fredricksburg until late afternoon. We reserved Monday and Tuesday for sightseeing but haven't done any of that yet. Something always seems to get in the way —motorhome washing, personal care (hair cuts, fingernails, etc), newsletter, handling our book business, being interviewed by local newspapers and so on. When we need to go into Austin (for the newsletter printing, etc), that takes a whole day. We think that this will be our last volunteer position for a while. We have loved it, and the people we meet and work with, but our book and newsletter business is enough work right now. Don't you think it is time we retired—at least a little bit?

♥ ⌂ ♥

7

GETTING READY

Since Ron was working and Barb wasn't, most of the getting ready was handled by Barb. She writes this chapter.

Ron and I talked about full-timing for so long that we can't really remember when, where, or exactly why we made the decision. Our "full-timing" talk was something that evolved slowly from our weekend camping trips, especially those taken the three years before we retired. We did a lot of talking those weekends. We talked while watching a sunrise, during walks, sitting at the beach, late at night around our private campfire and just after we retired to our motorhome bed. Always our talk was of how much we enjoyed this simple life and how we wished it could continue forever. Sundays were difficult because we had to face the reality of going home. On one of those homeward drives, we decided that when we retired, we would spend most of our time camping.

Ron and I attended a business conference in San Diego, California, one winter. It was our first trip to that part of the country. During our flight back to Michigan, we seriously began discussing all we could see when we were free to travel in our motorhome. Somewhere along the line, we realized that to see it all would take many years of summer vacations, or years of the longer trips we could take once retired. I think you are beginning to get the picture. One day we said, "There's so much to see, why not just live full time in the motorhome."

Since we had a few years to go before retirement, we began collecting data on this very different lifestyle. We honestly didn't know of anyone who lived full-time in a motorhome— not at first. And on every camping trip after that decision, we looked for those couples who were retirement age and asked lots of questions. We wanted to know if they kept their homes or just traveled a few months, where they went, if they knew any one who full-timed and so on.

We watched other campers, young and old, to see what kind of equipment they had, and we spent many hours discussing what our needs would be. For example, at first we said we wouldn't need to tow a car. I can't believe how naive we were. We never took a car on our camping weekends, and for alternative transportation, either biked or walked. We thought it would be too expensive and too much trouble buying a tow dolly and all. When we saw a motorhome pulling a car on all four wheels, we asked questions and discovered how easy that would be, and best of all, it wouldn't require a big investment since we could tow our old car.

At the time, we could find only one publication written about full-timing. We devoured *Trailer Life's Full-time RVing: A Complete Guide to Life on the Open Road*. We looked forward to our monthly issues of *Motorhome* and *Highways* which contained interesting information on camping and motorhomes, but little on full-timing.

From the time we made our decision to become full-timers, our weekend conversations became more like brainstorming. What will we do about clothing (won't need all those suits anymore)? Will we sell everything or put some things in storage? What little items out of the "junk" drawer will we need? Where will we go first? How will we get our mail? Should we cancel all of our magazine subscriptions? How can we get the most out of the storage space in our motor home? What about banking? What if one of us gets sick? And so on. It was fun to plan and explore all the possibilities. As we talked and thought, we began our serious planning.

Just as there are no two people who are alike, there will be no two couples who will think and act as we did. We knew our retirement date a full year ahead of time. Once we had that date (March 17, 1989), we picked the "take off" date. Since the lease on our town house ended on March 31, it seemed sensible to choose that date. We knew that just two weeks to complete all of our moving would be tight; but, with careful planning, it could be done. With paper and pencil, I worked out the schedule working backwards. The last two weeks looked like this:

March 17	Ron's last day at work
March 18	Our going away party
March 19	Finish packing
March 21	Movers move us into storage
March 22	Get ready for the sale
March 23-25	Moving sale
March 26	Easter
March 27-29	Clean, last minute details
March 30	Start our new life

Months before those last two weeks, I began packing one shelf, closet or bedroom at a time. I had five categories to sort to: (1) Save for storage; (2) Save for the moving sale; (3) Put in the motorhome; (4) Give to family/friends; (5) Throw away. Things for the moving sale were loosely put into boxes and set out of the way. I dealt with that closer to the 23rd. Boxes of possessions to be saved, were labeled, taped shut and stacked for the movers. Oh, and I began to take stock. I used to buy laundry soap, canned goods, etc., on sale and stock up. About six months before our take-off day, I happened to count the bars of bath soap I had on hand. I forget the exact number now, but when I calculated our usage, it came out that we had enough to last six months. I quit buying bath soap and lots of other things I had plenty of.

Since we were moving from a three-bedroom townhouse to a 24-foot Class C motorhome, deciding what to take and what to do with what is left took some thought. Most of us go through each day without thinking of the little things we have and use. My suggestion would be to start analyzing long before packing. For example, anytime an appliance was used, I asked myself, "Will I really need this?" "What is an alternative?" For me, some decisions were easy. I decided that instead of an electric can opener, a hand held old-fashioned one worked fine, took up little space and used no electricity. I could leave my electric mixer, toaster and coffee pot easily and use a wire whisk, griddle and old-fashioned stove top coffee pot instead. And I decided that I could live nicely without the microwave oven, especially when the alternative was more cupboard space. I personally think that mentally preparing for these changes early is important, otherwise the shock of leaving so many things behind could be overwhelming. If I had been moving into the 34-foot Bounder, I am sure I would have packed differently. I have lots of room now. I am sure I would have filled it to the brim—just like I did the Mallard. Now that we have experienced living without many of the things we previously thought we couldn't do without, I am content. I still don't want many of those things. There are exceptions, and I will cover those later, but let's continue packing the Mallard first.

When we first bought the little motorhome, we furnished it with new Corelle (difficult to break but like china) dinnerware. We also added new silverware and cookware because we wanted it to be special, and we didn't want to carry dishes and pans to the motorhome for every weekend trip. Although we would not need the dishes and other kitchen items from our house, we decided to keep them in storage for that time (if ever) when we quit full-timing. We carry service for four and find that is more than enough. When we do have company in campgrounds, it is usually other campers, and they bring their own coffee cup, etc. That's just the way it is done.

One of my most difficult decisions involved what staples to take. I love spices, and I love to cook. I decided that I could have all of my spices with me, if I had uniform sized containers. The brand I used most in my home had been *Spice Islands*. I like the bottles and found that 15 bottles would fit perfectly in a rectangular plastic container. With a waterproof marking pen, I wrote the name of each spice on the lid of the jar making for easy identification without removing the jars. Since all containers were the same height, I could place a second container with another 15 jars of spices on top of the first one. As a result, both fit nicely in the corner of one overhead cupboard. I did need to remove the whole container to see the spices, but I was willing to do that to have that luxury. The Bounder came with a handy spice rack which is part of the stove hood.

The overhead cupboards in most RVs are tall inside, so the stacking of plastic boxes, baskets and so on, enabled us to use the space more efficiently. I measured the length, depth and height, and spent hours at the housewares section of department stores, until I found the right combination for my cupboards.

I probably had 30 cookbooks at home, and I wondered how

I could carry all those books with me. I loved my cookbooks and didn't want to give them up. One day when I was following a favorite recipe from one of those books, I realized that there were only a half dozen favorites in that cookbook. That was the case in all of the books. It was an easy progression to see that all I had to do was copy those favorite recipes from each book onto a small file card before storing the cookbooks for some other day. An accordion recipe file book, which fits into an overhead cupboard, is only one inch wide and sure beats a lot of books. I don't have room for all those books in the Bounder either, so that solution is still a good one and works fine.

I had always prided myself on having a very organized kitchen and wanted my motorhome kitchen to be the same. I scaled it down to motorhome size. I used to buy 4 lbs. of brown sugar, 5 lbs. of granulated sugar, 5 lbs. of flour, 3 lbs. each of macaroni and rice, 3 lbs. of coffee, etc., and store it all in *Tupperware Modulars*. Now I buy 1 or 2 lbs. of most items and use small *Tupperware Modulars*. The *Tupperware Modulars* are square and rectangular which fit nicely in most RV cupboards. It is important to keep all these staples in air tight containers since we are so close to the out-of-doors. Foods in RVs are affected by dryness and humidity in addition to ants, roaches, etc. Those same containers fit beautifully in the Bounder's cupboards.

I have everything I need to fix most meals. I keep a small assortment of canned goods/staples on hand like spaghetti sauce, macaroni and cheese, soups and tuna. I know exactly how much our cupboards hold, and only buy what I can store. This same type of organization can be applied to the bathroom area. I used two small baskets to store the items that would normally be found in a medicine cabinet and placed them in a cupboard over the bed (we did not have a medicine cabinet in the Mallard). We each had a similar personal basket in our respective closets to hold things that might have been on our dressers. We now have a big medicine cabinet and many drawers in the Bounder. I do not need those baskets anymore.

Clothing was another difficult category. We had very little closet space in our motorhome so had to choose carefully. Ron picked out one suit, several ties, and two dress shirts. I picked one dress that is wrinkle free and two casual skirts with tops. I also added a dressy rayon three piece black suit. The skirt and loose fitting hip length jacket are perfect for any occasion and with the half dozen brightly colored silk shells I carry, it looks different each time I wear it. For a really special occasion, I wear the slacks and high heals with one of the shells and the jacket—it is very fashionable. The best part is that the three pieces hang on one hanger and the shells drape on one pant hanger.

These are our only good clothes. The rest of our wardrobe consists of tee shirts, sweat suits, jeans, shorts and bike shorts. We tried to be prepared for all kinds of weather. We were very careful in selecting just the right clothes and were never in serious need. I tried to choose easy-to-care-for clothing. Sometimes (like when we were in Vermont in the fall), we felt that we would never have enough warm clothing, but we managed by wearing the same clothes almost daily. If we skimped in any area it was cold weather clothing since we thought we would always be where it is warm. Even in West Palm Beach, Florida, on Christmas Eve, we were glad we had sweaters and coats. It got down to 28 degrees. I'm glad that we had to bring so little in the way of clothing at first. It made us realize how little we really need and we feel that is practical.

I like nice things and included all of my jewelry. By using two double sided fishing tackle boxes which measure 10" x 6" x 3", I was able to place them in the bottom corner of my closet. They hold all my earrings with room to add more. I like rings, bracelets, and long fingernails too. When I worked outside the home, I enjoyed the luxury of having my nails (acrylic) done every two weeks. When we knew we were going to be on the road, I asked my manicurist to teach me how to do my own. Now, every two weeks, I do my own nails. My hands do not look like a camper's hands because I take care of them. I wear makeup every day, so even if I am in shorts, I feel dressed up. I also made sure I had some sexy little nightgowns, black undergarments and my silk pillowcases.

Before we went on the road, I used to have candlelight dinners complete with wine, in crystal wine glasses. We did that—yes, even in our little 24 foot motorhome and plan to do that often in the Bounder too. This is me. There is no need to be different from the person you were before you started full-timing unless you want to.

In planning, we tried to think of every situation. When we returned to Michigan after our first year out, we went to our storage locker and traded some things. For example, Ron brought out his blue suit and temporarily retired his brown one. It was like we had brand new clothes.

Walk through your house and look at everything. What about the portraits on the wall, the little vase that Susie made in the fourth grade, the macrame owl Jim made, the anniversary clock that was a wedding gift, and all those special items that are so valuable to you? This is where it gets difficult and why we decided to rent a storage locker. We weren't ready to give up *everything*. We figured that the cost of a storage locker was worth our peace of mind, at least until we were sure we would really be happy as full-timers.

Some full-timers we have talked to use a family member's home attic for this purpose, thereby saving an expense, but we did not want to bother anyone. What if they move? We wanted to make the decision once and not worry about it again. Plus, we like our independence. We did make access arrangements for one son who lives near the locker. He can get things for us in an emergency or deposit additional items that we ship to him. We stored personal things that were important to us such as photos, gifts and a lot of little things that would be costly to replace if and when we settle down again.

We did keep a chest of drawers, a dresser, and a desk, in

order to store articles of clothing and some files in the drawers. Also in storage are three clothing wardrobes (the cardboard variety), my Hammond Organ, kitchen items (dishes, pots & pans, silverware, and small appliances), books, radios, phones and so on. No other furniture is stored. All of this will have changed by the time you read this though. When we have finished updating this book, we are heading back to Michigan to unload that storage locker and have a giant sale. I have written to all the kids, and asked what, if anything, they want. And there are a few things we will put into the Bounder. For example, I now have room for my *Electrolux* vacuum. We have been using a *Dirt Devil* for four years and it works great, but I am just a little tired of crawling around on my hands and knees to vacuum. Since we didn't have a microwave in the Mallard, I did not include any of my microwave dishes. Now I want them. The rest will be sold—once and for all.

We had a large record collection and decided to sell all of them at our moving sale after transferring the most precious ones to cassette tape. We carry those with us in the motorhome because the tapes are compact, easy to play and bring back lots of neat memories. This is another area where we are not giving up anything that we had at home. It just took a little planning and time to reduce the collection. Our tapes used to fit easily into two tape cases that stood up behind the motorhome driver's seat in what was, otherwise, wasted space. Now we have cupboard space for tapes.

We have everything that we need and lots we don't. Anything that we don't use in one year, will be thrown out or given away. We have Elmer's glue, cellophane tape, paper clips, safety pins, a tape measure, magnifying glass, pens, pencils, stamps, envelopes, screwdrivers, pliers, clothespins, and brown packaging tape to mention some small articles. The trick is organizing these items into a limited space. We also have golf clubs, tennis rackets, bicycles, panniers (bicycle saddle bags), bike equipment, a tool box, and cooler to mention some of the bigger objects. These items used to fit in the towed vehicle or the storage pod on the roof of the motorhome. Now we have plenty of room in the basement compartments.

Although we had camped nearly every summer weekend over a three year period, and each cupboard had been packed, we had to redo it all for full-timing. We had not made the best use of space.

Cab Over Storage In Lieu Of Bed

The Mallard was a class C which means that it had a bed over the cab area. We decided that we could remove the mattress and use milk crates—three on each side—to hold such items normally found in dresser drawers. With the help of *Scoot Guard* (a textured rubbery material which keeps objects from sliding around) these crates traveled well and even when full actually weighed less than the mattress we removed. *Scoot Guard* is available in most camper stores and is valuable when used in cupboards too. The mattress was put in storage so we could replace it if and when we sold the motorhome. But when we traded the Mallard for the Bounder, we were in Florida and the mattress was in Michigan. The dealer didn't care if we had the mattress or not and did not depreciate the trade in price. We needn't have saved it and now will sell it outright.

We made room for a box of our favorite games. This box fit in that area over the cab in the Mallard and under the sofa in the Bounder. We have never been bored, even when we have been rained in for two or three days. *Scrabble, Rummicube, Yahtzee, Cribbage*, playing cards, *Uno, Score Four, Chess, Othello, Chinese Checkers, Dominos and Backgammon* are the games we carry. The Christmas before we started full-timing presented a problem with Christmas gifts. We were getting rid of possessions and neither one of us wanted to think of adding to our material goods, so Ron and I agreed to buy each other one game to add to our game box. It had to be small and under $10. That was a fun Christmas and we still enjoy those games.

We had family photos (in miniature) displayed in frames over the entry door. This idea was picked up from a neat couple we met in the Smoky Mountains National Park. Lola and Harold were campground hosts at the Elkmont campground there, and they had the twin to our motorhome. It was fun to see how they had decorated their house, and we copied several ideas from them. Lola had her family pictures over the door in a small but very usable space. When we were near a store, I purchased little frames and made an attractive homey arrangement. I just hadn't thought of using any of the wall space until then. Now, our photos are on an attractive shelf (window ledge high and wide) behind the couch—Fleetwood thought of everything.

Both Ron and I like to read. I am still amazed at all the little spaces that I was able to find and fill. Behind our swivel barrel chair there was a perfect little space for a cardboard magazine box, and it held about nine paperbacks. They didn't roll around, were easy to reach, and were completely out of the way. For magazines, in the Mallard, we found a magazine rack at a camping store and it fit perfectly on the wall space just inside the entry door. We have book shelves and two magazine racks now. We don't collect books so after we read them, we look for used book stores where they take books in partial trade for other used books, or we simply leave them in campground lounges.

Helpful Magazines

The question of where to go on our travels intrigued us. We wanted to go everywhere. We had been getting *Motorhome* magazine for well over two years and had all the magazines stacked on a book shelf. We had read much about many interesting places, yet couldn't remember anything specific. There was no way that we could carry all those books, and the cookbook solution came to mind. I bought *Pendeflex* hanging files and labeled one for each of the continental United States, Canada, Mexico, miscellaneous, and motor home maintenance. It took many winter evenings (another reason for starting to prepare in advance) for me to

Our Travel Bibles

go through each magazine, clip the articles and put each in the appropriate file. The file is stored in three separate topless *Rubbermaid* file boxes that take up very little space and are invaluable. As we enter a new state, we get out the respective file and make our plans from the articles in the file. When we collect state maps, they also go into the appropriate file. It was a lot of fun to go through the files—as we neared our departure day—and talk about where we were going to go. It is easy to keep up our file now. After we have thoroughly read each magazine, I clip the articles and add them to the file. Once the articles are clipped, we can throw out the magazine. We collect those "tourist" brochures as we enter a state or area, but not for long. Once we leave a state, we clean out the file by giving most of the brochures to a fellow camper who may be going where we have been. We keep the magazine articles until we visit that area, and the maps are kept until they fall apart.

The file is also a good place to store newspaper articles on local places of interest. This is how we found out about *Mother's*, a fantastic restaurant in New Orleans, specializing in PO Boy sandwiches. We first read about this place in *USA today*, but we were in Mississippi and would have forgotten all about it had it not been entered in our file.

Another item in each file is very special to us. We had a party to coincide with our retirement and the commencement of our full-timing. We asked each of our guests to bring a 3 x 5 card with their name and address on one side and a description of their favorite place to visit in the continental U.S., on the other side. These we added to the respective state files, so that when we enter a state, we see the card, visit the spot and send a post card thank you to our friend. It has been a lot of fun to keep in touch with our friends this way.

I credit the success of our planning to the fact that Ron and I talked and talked and talked. We tried to think of every situation that could come up and discussed what we would do. For example, what would we do if a family member became critically ill and we had to get to them in a hurry? We added compact, fold flat luggage to our pod, and now if we ever need to fly, we have luggage. We decided to carry our medical records with us in the event that we needed medical care. These are also easy to come by and take up little space.

Part of our planning involved modifying our motorhome. The original foam mattress was not holding up. Since it was the kind with a corner cut off, we knew we would have to special order a new one. We shopped at a fine furniture store and chose extra firm foam. Although it seemed expensive at the time ($300), it has been worth every penny spent. When we traded motorhomes, I really felt sad leaving our wonderful mattress. With its 12-year warranty, it was still like new. We loved it so much that we have ordered a queen sized one from the same company and will pick it up when we get back to Michigan. We also shopped for a tow bar for the car, a storage pod for the top of the motorhome, and a bike rack for the roof of the car.

The rest of the planning involved locating a mail forwarding service, ordering an AT&T calling card, sending out the change of address cards, arranging for a storage locker, finding movers, setting a date for the moving sale, and actually moving. Anyone who has ever moved will recognize a lot of these same steps. I noticed one major difference. I had to be very careful to use perishable items before the move. Normally when moving, one carries cleaning products and food from the freezer, refrigerator, and cupboards to the new house. I couldn't do that. Since we wouldn't need most of the cleaning products (you don't use scouring powders or Draino, etc., in an RV), I either used them up or gave them away and the same with excess perishable goods.

I could go on and on with the little details, but I am sure that our life is different from yours and some things might not apply. Try to take your hobbies with you. Good friends of ours have unique hobbies and carry them along. Liz was a quilting teacher so she has all her materials and sewing machine with her. Her husband, Don, is a ham radio operator and found room for all that equipment plus a scanner and a computer in his fifth-wheel. Your life shouldn't change drastically when you become a full-timer.

We have changed our thoughts on some things since we started out. But we wouldn't have done it any other way.

If I had to condense this chapter into a single sentence, it would be, "Plan, think and talk—over and over again—then talk about it some more. While you're at it, make lots of lists too."

♥   ♥

From my Diary

Wednesday, February 1, 1989, We are really counting down. Ron said this morning, "I can now say that next month I'll be retired."

Thursday, February 3, 1989, Mailed out change of address forms to all our magazines.

Saturday, February 4, Well, the couch is gone, as well as coffee table, lamp, drapes, etc. Robert was so excited to have these things for his apartment. He also took my painting table and all of Jim's boxes to his father's. Played Pinochle with Jim and Norma in the evening. Fun!

Monday, February 6, 1989, Went to the Spa. Tough! Picked up stuff from Speedy Printing (invitations and moving notice). I like the notices—good thing Sherrie (at Speedy) helped me. Worked on the afghan—want to have it done in time for Friday and my lunch with Carolyn. It's her big 4-0.

Tuesday, February 7, Care called—changed lunch to TOMORROW! Worked steadily all day and evening until 11:30 p.m.— finally finished. WOW!

Wednesday, February 8, 1989, Went to the spa, then had a nice lunch with Care. She loved the afghan. Got my perm and the instructions to carry with me. Hope I find others as good as Debbie.

Thursday, February 9, Picked up the business cards, moving notices. Cute! Closed out my account at Hudson's, addressed our invitations and packed the downstairs wall hangings [pictures]. The place looks naked.

Saturday, February 11, 1989, I cleaned the basement while Ron was at the spa. Shopped at Gordon's Food Service to get some things for our party. Went to dinner with Jim and Norma (Mountain Jack's) then came back here and played Pinochle. I didn't feel real good—tired.

Monday, February 13, 1989, At 4 a.m. Ron took me to ER. Fever, chills—hurt all over. Thought I had pneumonia—they said bronchitis. Came home and slept all day.

Friday, February 17, 1989, One month from today, Ron retires. I've spent this week resting and resting. Haven't even been outside. Lungs still scratchy. I'm crabby—want to exercise and resume normal activities. Yesterday, I cleaned out the desk and was tired.

Saturday, February 18, 1989, Felt much better

Monday, February 20, 1989, Ron is off—Presidents Day. We took the car to Dennis Trailer Sales to have the tow bar put on. Ate breakfast out. We priced some of our sale stuff.

Wednesday, February 22, I bought Jackie a nice scarf and pin and took it to her for teaching me to do my nails. We cried as we hugged "goodby." She's my first "goodby." I know I'll cry a river when the time comes to leave everything.

Friday, February 24, E Gads!! Three weeks to go. Ron has a cold, and I'm tired. I wake up early every a.m. and can't go back to sleep for thinking. I'm worrying that our full-time life will be awful—that I'll miss not having a home to come home to. I suppose this is normal.

Monday, March 6, It was a slow week. I didn't do any big thing. All our pictures are down and packed. I took a bunch of our clothes to the cleaners. Now they're packed in a wardrobe box—for storage. Couldn't pick up the motorhome Sat—ice storm—We will wait till next Sat. It will be warmer. Meanwhile, we wait.

Friday, March 10, We got the motorhome. They completed the hookup for the tow bar. Ron drove the motorhome and the car home. I followed in the company car. It looked so cute to see the car being pulled. Right away we took down the sheets that I had covering the windows and made a clever box for under the bed—to hold shoes. We put the new mattress out there. Wow!!! It's a thick wonderful mattress.

Saturday, March 11, We filled the pod. Can't believe it holds so much. Fantastic. I've been planning cupboard storage—put towels (rolled) under the sink. I think that will be efficient. Jim and Norma came and took the big hanging plant from the kitchen. Kitchen looks so empty now. Went to Jim's for chili and pinochle after we shopped at the mall for two more milk crates. Took the mattress from the cab bunk out of the motorhome and will use that space, as is, for six milk crates filled with clothes, and an under-the-bed type box filled too.

Sunday, March 12, 1989, Did more moving and sorting.

Monday, March 13, 1989, Wow—did I work. Food—cupboards—clothes—cleared off my dresser and Ron's too—just did a bunch. Also returned the cable. Ron cleaned off the desk.

Sunday, March 19, 1989, Ron's retirement luncheon (Thursday the 16th) was great. 150 were there, and when it was over we felt a little lost. Then the next day was his last at work. He said people filed into his office all day. I picked him up at 4:30 (no more state car). It was the beginning of an ice storm. We came straight home. I had been shopping and cutting veggies, etc., all day, and we did more at night. Woke up Saturday morning to ICE—thick and everywhere. It took Ron a long time to chisel the ice off his car to get in. Then he got to the club house, and that door wouldn't open. Once we got going though, things progressed nicely. The party was a big success.

Monday, March 20, Packed all day. Tired.

Tuesday, March 21, The movers came at noon and were done by four. Now we have one day to get ready for the moving sale. We are sleeping on the floor in our bedroom. There is nothing much left in the house, but it is too cold to sleep out in the motorhome.

Tuesday, March 28, Last night I made a new recording for our answering machine. It says, "Hi!, this is Barb. Ron and I are home, but home now is our motorhome parked out in the parking lot. So if you'd like to see us—come on over—we'd love the company. Otherwise leave a message at the sound of the tone and we will check it in the morning when we come in the house." Yes, we're un-winterized and everything is moved in. We had filled the motorhome so full that I was worried we were overweight. But Ron had her weighed and we can still add 1,500 pounds. Whoopee!!

Wednesday March 29, Poor Ron has the flu. Since Ron is sick, I made the last trip to the storage locker. We were scheduled to go to dinner with Jim and Norma and did, but Ron left early and went home. I cried when we hugged and said "good-by". Oh, I checked for messages on our voice mail today. It is so fantastic. I love it. It will make full-timing easy.

Thursday, March 30, It's cold and yukky. We got our business done—car loaded, bikes on top. Ron went to the credit union while I went to the laundromat. That done, we put water in the motorhome, hooked up the car and turned in our town house keys. I cried a little saying, "goodby," to Carol and leaving the house. Then I was fine. Ron seemed so relaxed. It was good to finally be starting our new life.

♥ △ ♥

Beginning Our New Life

Snapshots

Camden, Maine Harbor
Ron Eating Lobster
Ron Loading His Bus

Barb Leading A Tour At Hot Springs National Park
Ron & Look Alike MM At Universal Studios
Golfing In Florida
Our House Takes A Ferry Ride

Oatman, Arizona,
Montezuma Well
NHP—Arizona,
Bryce Canyon,
Utah

Snow In Yosemite National Park, California
Crater Lake National Park, Oregon
Mirror Lake, Yosemite National Park, California
Redwoods National Park, California

Firy Furnace Hike At Arches National Park, Utah
Ghost Town In Montana
Arches National Park, Utah

Bodie, A Ghost Town in Northern California
North Cascades National Park, Washington
Panning For Gold In A Montana Ghost Town
Luckenbach, Texas

Yellowstone National Park, Wyoming
Mt. Rainier National Park, Washington
Mt. St. Helen National Forest, Washington
Canyonlands National Park, Utah (The Trail We Biked)

Davis Mountians State Park, Texas
Ron & His Mom Walking At The LBJ Ranch
At The Rose Bowl—Pasedena, California
Grandchildren Mary & Richard Roasting Marshmallows In The Rain

Ron At The Excalibur Casino, Las Vegas, Nevada
Barb Moving From One House To Another

Liisa On Top Of Sentinel Dome (With Half Dome In The Background)—
Yosemite National Park, California
Barb & Charlie Chaplain Look Alike At Universal Studios, California
Barb And Son Robert On The Coast Guard Cutter, Sherman—
Oakland, California

8

ON THE ROAD

Keeping In Touch

We have nine children (it is a second marriage), 15 grand-children, two living mothers, one living father, seven sisters, and one brother between us. We also have aunts, uncles and many special friends. We didn't want to abandon any of them. It was, and is, very important that we keep in touch with family and friends. Therefore, we carefully chose reliable mail forwarding and voice mail services.

Mail Forwarding

From the "service" advertisements in *Motorhome* magazine

and *Highways*, we wrote to all the mail forwarding services asking for information. Most work on the same principle—mail is received and saved until you notify the company when and where to send it. The mail is then packaged in a large envelope and sent out. The forwarding service charges a monthly fee and works from a deposit for re-mailing postage. We made our decision on their presentation and price. We happened to pick a service whose primary business was providing a financial district address for those who worked out of their home in that state. They had little experience with full-timers and their constant moving.

We managed for nearly two years, then our service was sold, and things got very bad. Now we know how frustrating it can be to have an unsatisfactory mail service. After suffering for six months we changed to *Escapees Mail and Message Service* and are very pleased with both the service and their professionalism. They are used to dealing with full-timers and it shows. Our first mail service cost us $80 per year plus postage. Escapees minimum charge is $62 plus postage and a $40 per year membership fee which gives us other benefits. In checking other mail service prices we found they vary widely.

Many full-timers use family for their mail service. We decided against that for several reasons. They all lead busy lives and don't need to be worrying about our mail. If they move we would have to go to the trouble of sending out change of address notices. The main reason we wanted to use a professional service was to have full control.

Many RV organizations such as *Good Sam and Family Motor Coach Association FMCA),* offer a mail service. When we checked, we found that they have some restrictions. FMCA, for example, controls when mail can be sent out. For example, if your name begins with an "H," mail can only be sent out on Tuesdays. We wanted to be able to call any day to request mail. Another service indicated that they would not be able to handle a weekly change in addresses. That would be fine if we were spending a whole season in one place.

Some services insist that all requests for re-mailing be mailed in to their office. That means we would have to know in advance where we are going and when we will get there. We don't travel like that.

Some full-timers get small amounts of mail so only need mail sent once a month if that often. We get lots of mail and like it sent to us every week. We generally have our mail sent in care of General Delivery at a small post office near where we will be staying. Once, we made the mistake of receiving mail in Las Vegas. Never again! They have a window just for general delivery and short hours of operation. We had to stand in line for nearly an hour. Las Vegas has many transients. When a post office receives your mail they will hold it for two weeks and if you don't claim it in that time, they will return it. Having mail sent several days to a week before you expect to be traveling through will also work. Just stop in at the post office on your way. If family will be handling your mail for you, suggest that they use the Priority envelopes that the post office furnishes. They are tear proof, large and free.

Message and Voice Mail Services

In an emergency we wanted to be able to be contacted, but we didn't want to have to call someone in the family every time we moved to a different campground to give them the new phone number. We didn't want to have to make an itinerary and stick to it. We also wanted family to be able to call and leave a non-emergency message—just to keep in touch. Investigating, we discovered a variety of message services available to the full-timer. As in the mail service, some large RV associations provide this service too. The fees range from free to costly.

FMCA offers a free *Emergency* message service which recently changed from a "human" to computer-generated service. They do stress that it is for emergency use only and provide an 800 number. This is great for family, and we like knowing that we will hear the caller's voice rather than someone relaying a message. We currently use this service but have had a few concerns. There are a lot of numbers to punch in after reaching the 800 number, and our elderly parents got confused. Those who have left messages say that they are never really sure if they are leaving the message for us. They want to hear our voice greeting them. During peak snowbird travel times (spring and fall) when many are using the service, the line can be busy for hours. We understand that FMCA is trying to alleviate this problem. You must have a motorhome to belong to FMCA.

Good Sam offers a good Voice Mail service. This too is computer-generated, but it is more like a regular phone answering machine to someone calling in. The service, which costs $11.95 per month plus 29 cents per minute of usage, offers an 800 number. Once signed up, you are given an extension number which becomes your personal number. To start with, you would put a message on your service much like you did at home. When anyone calls they will hear your message and be directed to "leave a message at the tone." This number is available 24 hours a day.

We subscribed to a voice mail service in Denver, Colorado, from the beginning and have been very happy with it. *Voice Tel. of Colorado* works basically the same as the Good Sam service except it does not provide an 800 number. It does have a toll saver feature though. If, when we call, it rings a certain number of times, we know there are no messages and we hang up. We do not have to pay for a phone call and know that we have no messages—"the coast is clear." Our monthly charge is $16 and would work out about the same as the Good Sam service when per minute extra charges are addded in. With the Good Sam service, the 29 cent per minute charge is added every time one checks the service and twice for messages—once when they are left and again when they are retrieved.

Since we can call anytime to check on messages and know there will only be a charge if there is a message, we call every evening between seven and nine p.m. (eastern time). Everyone knows that is our check-in time. We have assured family that we will never be out of touch for more than 24 hours and think this is comforting to them. Since our messages are left on a recording, we get the exact message that is left and there is no chance of notes being misplaced or messages confused by a personal answering service.

For those just looking for the basics, several credit card companies offer an emergency message service at very low rates. Discover, for example charges under $10 per year for a "human" message service. Those who do not like computers might enjoy this, but the several times we have left messages on the Discover service we were a bit frustrated. For example, we got a message on our service from friends who had just purchased a new Bounder and were on their way to visit us. We wanted to say, "Wow, that's great," and so on. We did, but knew it lost a lot of expression while we were relaying it word-by-word to the person typing the message. We could just imagine how dry it was when being repeated. But, at least, we were able to communicate, and that was the important thing.

Some people prefer to use an expensive cellular phone but complain that in many parts of the country it simply doesn't work. When it does work, it is very expensive.

Another alternative is just to check with family periodically (usually once a week). But what happens in between? A couple we met in Mississippi made their weekly phone call home to find that the family had been frantically looking for them since the last phone call one week before. It seems that right after the weekly check-in phone call a grandchild went to the hospital seriously ill, and the grandparents couldn't be found.

To be honest, we have received few messages and were glad to get each one. We have learned about the birth of grand-children (six since we began full-timing), the death of a friend, and family wedding plans to name a few. Occasionally someone will call just because they want to talk to us. We like that feature.

There is one difficult facet of the computer-generated services. They require a touch tone phone. In some remote areas of this country we may be miles from a touch tone phone. In the northern Michigan town of Grand Marais, we discovered we had a message but couldn't find a touch tone phone. We learned that the nearest one was 25 miles away. After pleading with telephone supervisors, we finally got one to help us, but he didn't stay on the phone long enough. He got us into the service then left before we could play the message. We had to go through that pleading again (three times that night) before we finally got our messages.

The next time we were in a big city, we bought a phone dialer which simulates the touch tone, and that has saved us more than once. The telephones are not uniform like they once were, and with all the different long distance companies and their problems, telephoning is probably our biggest negative in full-timing.

Do you and your spouse like to be on the phone at the same time when talking to family members? That is OK while you still have your home and extensions, but you will not find that feature on pay phones. The good news is that for about $10 at most Radio Shack stores, you can purchase a phone listener. It is very simple. A suction cup attached to the side of the ear piece transmits the conversation to a small speaker. You won't be able to talk at the same time, but at least you can both listen at the same time.

The Birth of *Movin' On*

We prepared everyone for our new lifestyle well in advance. Our Christmas letter—just three months before our move—told of all the excitement in planning and packing, and mentioned that soon we would send out our new address. We actually acquired our mail service a full two months before we

We're Moving...

          Moving...

                    Moving...

Ron & Barb Hofmeister
101 Rainbow Dr.
Apt. 2179
Livingston, TX 77351-9300

Our Business Card

needed it because we wanted to give the address out to those businesses and organizations we would continue to work with. We also made a cute moving notice and sent it out to all our family and friends. Using the same design, we had business cards made so we could hand them out to the many new friends we would meet along the way.

New return address labels were ordered, and we made a stationery box out of a white cardboard box available at many shops specializing in boxes. It is compact (10 ½" x 12" x 2 ½"), has a hinged top and holds note paper, envelopes, stamps, and even a hand-held computerized dictionary/thesaurus. Since the box is self-contained, it can ride anywhere in the motorhome, and when we are writing, we can move it out to the picnic table or set it next to us at the dinette.

At first, letters were fun to write—we were eager to share all of our experiences with everyone. With so many to write to, it didn't take long before we got writer's cramp and became bored with writing the same information over and over again. But, we had promised everyone that we would keep in touch. Writing became much easier after we purchased a laptop computer and a printer. We cheated a lot—wrote the travel information and copied that to each letter. Just the beginning and the end of each letter were personalized. We tried to kid ourselves that no one knew what we were really doing.

The first Christmas on the road, we used the computer to make a Christmas letter to send to all of our friends and family. That turned out so well that we decided to publish a monthly newsletter and let that carry our travel and lifestyle news.

We used a primitive (and difficult to use) software program to create our first newsletter. It was the front and back of one page, and we sent out 30 copies to family and a few close friends. It was fun to make the newsletter and even with stamps and envelopes, the cost was under $10. The comments we got were very positive, and we started gathering information for the second issue. By the second issue, we had changed to a better software program and added an extra page. But we only printed on one side of that extra page. Instead of using an envelope, we tri-folded the newsletter and used the blank back page for the address, etc. Two issues later we were using three pages, again keeping the back page blank, giving us five pages for copy. We got really fancy when we started using our Word Perfect software and detailed graphics. Now we have the maximum number of pages we can mail for one stamp—nine and one half pages of copy.

Gradually we added features. When people started sending letters with comments on the articles, we printed excerpts in a *Letters* section; a *Coast to Coast Update* reviewed the campgrounds we stayed at that month; *This' n That* and *Potpourri* contained tidbits of information on a variety of subjects; *Interesting People* brought to life some of the new friends we met; then *Family News* dealt with personal items that non-family members might not be interested in. We also added photographs and lots of graphics to help illustrate the stories.

As we met new friends, we handed out our most recent newsletter. Suddenly we had over 100 on our mailing list and believe that they all enjoy receiving the paper. We had to ask

Some of Our Newsletters

for postage from our friends to help alleviate the cost which was well over $100 per month. When the subscription list continued to grow, we decided to freeze our old friends at a stamp per issue while family remained free. New friends needed to pay $1.50 per issue. We now print 500 copies of each newsletter, and the mailing list is still growing. It gives us pleasure.

We don't always publish each month but do promise six issues per year. We reserve the right to do monthly issues as we feel the need, keeping it loose, but it does make doing business complicated. Our subscribers order a certain number of issues (however many they want) and send the appropriate amount of money. Each time we mail out an issue the number in the upper left corner of the mailing label decreases. When the number gets to zero (meaning they have no more issues paid for), they can send more money or be taken off the mailing list.

All in all—keeping in touch has been fun. We haven't lost track of any of our friends or family. In fact, we are communicating more with our old friends and have added many new, wonderful friends. Full-timers become an extended family and it has been a joy to keep in touch with each and every one.

♥ ♥

From the October 1991 issue of Movin' On

TRAVEL TIPS ARE FUN

Everyone has a place that they remember as "the most interesting" or "the most beautiful" in all of the United States, so we asked our friends to list this place on a 3 x 5 card, and bring it to the party we had two weeks before we began full-timing.

Everyone cooperated and most even included names of places to eat or things to do in the area. We filed all of these cards in the appropriate state file that we carry with us. And as we are about to enter each new state, we get out the file and see what articles we have saved and what 3 x 5 cards, if any, are there. When we visit "the spot," we pick up a post card and send it off with a thank you.

There are a few that we have missed so far. Chuck Fisher suggested Monterey Bay, California, but all of you know that we didn't do much touring in California because of the brown bomb (our old car). I don't have the California file

out, but I know we missed a few others too. The cards are still there, and we will visit those places yet.

We are pleased to mention that the ones we have visited have been wonderful, and in most cases we would have entirely missed the experience if it weren't for our good friends' suggestions.

Our first "card" visits were to the Finger Lakes region in upstate New York, and the charming town of Weston, VT. Recently, visits to Sedona, Arizona, Crater Lake, Oregon, Sandpoint, Idaho, and Jackson Hole, Wyoming, were a direct result of the cards. It was fun.

If we haven't visited your place yet, the card is still in the file. We will get there someday. For those of you who have joined us since we have been on the road, please feel free to jot down *that special place* on a 3 x 5 card, send it to us and we will do our best to get there.

From The December 1992 Issue of Movin' On

TELEPHONE

TALK

Full-timers need a reliable telephone service, and we happen to like AT&T. Some small telephone companies try to lock out AT&T customers, forcing them to use their terrible and expensive service. But AT&T fixed that. First of all if the pay phone you are attempting to use does not use AT&T, try dialing 10-ATT (288) - 0 then your number. If that doesn't work, and it happens more often than we like to think about, dial 1-800-CALL-ATT, listen to the recording and follow instructions. If you are trying to make a credit card call, you will be asked to punch 1; for a collect call press 2, etc. After that, you may proceed to dial all the numbers. Yes, it seems like a lot of work, but it does work.

Last month I wrote about the new "Call and Save" plan offered by AT&T. But I kept referring to the "calling card" as a credit card. It was pointed out to me that AT&T does, in fact, have a Universal Visa Card which allows one to make regular credit card purchases anywhere and make charge calls too. More than one told me that they receive a 10% discount on their phone calls with this card.

After checking with AT&T, I learned that the 10% discount with the Universal Card was only for charter card holders and is not offered any longer. If you already have one—great.

The Calling Card that we have is not a credit card. It is strictly for telephone calls. With the new "Call and Save" program, the savings are good to great depending on when you call—5% daytime, 10% evening, 20% nights and weekends. Remember you don't have to have a telephone to get either card. If you have any questions, call AT&T at 1-800-CALL ATT. They are very helpful.

From the January 1993 issue of Movin' On

COFFEE BREAK

Take a break. Get a cup of coffee and let's chat.

I can't make my mother understand how mail forwarding works. She seems to think that she has to write to us where we are instead of our service. Can you help say it in a way she can understand? Kay M, Merced, CA

I'll try. When you decide that you will need mail forwarding, whether it is family or a professional service, choose the family member or service you are going to use. Notify everyone you get mail from of your new address. Your mail goes to the new address where they hold it for you. Then, at your request, they will put it all in a large envelope and mail it to you wherever you are. Most people choose a small town post office and have the mail sent to General Delivery. The post office will hold General Delivery mail for two weeks so if it gets there before you do they will hold it.

We did not want to bother family, since they are all very busy, so we went straight to a professional service.

I don't know if I answered your question, but perhaps if I describe what goes on at a service it will help. I have just seen, first hand, how one of the best mail forwarding services works, and it certainly impressed me.

Escapees Mail and Message Service is obviously doing something right because they have grown from two subscribers to over 3,000 in just a few short years. Members use the same address (101 Rainbow Drive) and their own number which is essential with such a large number of subscribers. Mail comes in by the carload and is first sorted by number into large categories.

Each subscriber has a hanging file, and the second step is to put each piece of mail in the proper file. Several employees do nothing but sort mail all day long.

The biggest problem is mail that arrives without a number. Each piece has to be checked against the master computer list to find the number so it can be sorted. This delays mail for a minimum of one day and is a full time job for at least one employee.

Two women take the many phone calls and directions for re-mailing the mail while a couple of other workers spend their day pre-paring the mail to be sent out. Each subscriber has specific in-structions (save catalogs, throw out catalogs, send 1st class mail priori-ty, send magazines separately, etc.) which have to be followed when preparing the mail to be forwarded.

Certainly Escapees MMS is not the only service available, but in my book, it is the best.

♥ ⌂ ♥

9

ON THE ROAD
Handling Finances

One of the first questions we get asked by people not familiar with our lifestyle has to do with money. "How do you get it?" "Do you use traveler's checks?" Actually, handling finances on the road is really quite simple because of the proliferation of automated teller machines (ATMs) found even in small towns. By using ATMs we are now able to take our bank with us, because we are never more than an ATM away. If intimidated by computers, including an ATM, one is not alone. We find, however, that full-timers take on challenges and will soon discover that these high speed adding machines are really not very complicated. They can be a tremendous help anywhere, anytime. Full-timers can function on the road without an ATM card, but it will be more time consuming and involve some service charges when using the more traditional methods.

It is helpful if your bank or credit union is a full service banking institution. If not, consider changing to one that is. Since we are on the move constantly, direct deposits, checking accounts, saving accounts, loan accounts, and transfers between these accounts are best handled by transactions with the same institution through ATMs. Even without using ATMs, it is easier to deal with one banking institution on a long distance basis. It may be preferable to use another institution or brokerage for savings and/or investments, but these funds should then be transferred as needed by direct deposit into the full service account. Those funds can then be accessed by ATM as needed for cash flow purposes.

The full-timer will quickly note that each state has different ATM networks within that state. Accessing these networks can be done through any bank associated with that particular network. Most banking institutions have established reciprocal arrangements with other networks. We were pleased to learn that our credit union has agreements with many networks across the country. Depending on which state we are in, and the availability of member banks, we are never far from a ready cash source. Although we have found that most private and public campgrounds accept personal checks, this method of payment is not often accepted when making purchases in a strange town.

On one occasion we were thankful to have our check accepted. In the remote town of Grand Marais, Michigan, situated on the shores of Lake Superior, and miles from nowhere, there were no ATMs to be found. For that matter, we couldn't access our funds manually through a bank clerk, because the bank was not connected to a banking network. Not to worry—the bank simply cashed our checks. When we offered to produce identification, the clerk said it wouldn't be necessary. Such is life in a small town.

Checks, of course, are good for mailing payments to a company where a business relationship has been established. To avoid carrying large amounts of cash, we find it convenient to use several credit cards including a telephone calling card. Credit card charges are then paid by check regularly to avoid interest charges. We have found that the grace period for payment is sufficient even when using our mail forwarding service. If there is concern about receiving and paying the account balance before an interest charge is added, it is possible to keep a credit balance on the card by paying more than what's owed. This works well with small accounts such as gasoline credit cards. Obviously, it's not a good idea to prepay large amounts because the funds would not earn interest.

Another method that many find efficient is the debit charge card. On this type of arrangement, the purchase is immediately charged through the use of a special card to a savings balance that earns interest. Periodic direct mail deposits can replenish this account, and many banks offer the service.

Because of credit established before we began our nomadic life, we have not had problems with credit card companies. When we explain our lack of a telephone and the use of a mail forwarding service, they seem to understand. Once our Visa renewal card was delayed when another bank bought out the operation. When we explained to the new bank that we use the card for daily expenses, they mailed the new card to us using overnight mail.

To keep it simple, we use only one major credit card, one major oil company card and a telephone calling card besides our ever useful ATM card. The oil company card may not be necessary since most gasoline stations accept major credit cards in addition to their own. But it is comforting to have in case of major repairs or tire purchases.

Most people think that it's necessary to have a telephone in order to obtain a telephone calling card. Not so, but it's best to apply for one while still having a credit history with the telephone company. At first, our full-timing telephone bill was averaging $60 a month. We found that our $100 telephone calling card limit was not sufficient. By the time our payment was received, current charges were already in the system. We could have prepaid and kept a credit balance with the telephone company, but a telephone call immediately established a new limit at $300.

Credit cards can also be used in ATMs for a ready cash source called cash advances. If ATMs are intimidating, the credit card can still be the alternative way of obtaining cash by presenting the card to a bank honoring the card. This can be done by going directly to a teller, so an ATM is not required. Cash advances, whether by ATM or through a bank teller, are best paid by check upon receiving the statement (or even before) to avoid interest. Usually there is a small service charge.

If credit cards and ATM cards are undesirable to some, many banks will cash personal checks after a short waiting period. This may work when staying in the same area for a while. Some full-timers prefer to use traveler's checks, however, these tie up funds without interest and have a nominal charge. Whatever method used, potential full-timers should know that obtaining cash on the road is not difficult and should not be a concern. Most of the methods work best when the income source is directly deposited to a banking institution of choice—preferably a full service bank.

So, if paying bills and obtaining ready cash is no problem on the road, what is needed in the way of funds? Chapter 10 may give some help in developing a budget or a beginning spending plan. Besides a budget, we found it helpful to prepare a cash flow schedule covering a period of 18 months. By looking at this time span we could see if retirement income matched outgo both in the short and long term. It was important for us to know if severance pay would hold us until retirement checks started arriving or if we would need to use savings. We knew that we would have some start up costs, but there would be some offsetting revenue because of moving sales, recouping security deposits, etc. It was important for us to see on paper exactly how the cash would flow, hence, a cash flow projection. Once accomplished, it was surprising how this eased our minds and allowed us to concentrate on the adventurous part of full-timing.

Projected monthly income has to be the cornerstone of the cash flow statement. Monthly income includes pensions, annuities, interest, social security, rental income, land contract income, or any other source of income received. It is not our purpose here to analyze investment programs or suggest alternative plans, only to recognize those income sources as an integral part of cash flow planning. For some the income may be only social security, or it could include estimated part time wages. Although we have been discussing retirement type planning, younger full-timers also need to work with cash flow projections as they deal with a different set of problems and income sources.

The second step in preparing a cash flow schedule is identifying monthly expenditures. In preparing cash flow schedules, some like to amortize or spread out large payments made for items such as insurance, license plates and membership fees. In our opinion, it is helpful to do this in planning a budget, but for cash flow purposes, it is best to include the actual cash outlay in the month that it occurs. By doing this, periods may be identified (hopefully not too many) where cash outlays will exceed income. Planning ahead (saving) in the easy months, or temporary withdrawals from savings, will insure that cash is available to meet those large expenses that, thankfully, don't occur every month. Expenditure planning will fall into three categories—fixed, variable and discretionary. Let's look at the three categories.

The easiest part of preparing a cash flow statement is identifying fixed expenses (Figure 6) because we know what they are. Although RV payments are included here as an expense, in a strict accounting sense they are not, but rather the

Insurance
License Plates
RV Payments
Storage
Membership Fees

Figure 6   Fixed Expenses

retirement of a debt. Like mortgage payments, they need to be recognized in cash flow planning. It makes sense when considering that the RV is now the home. Another major fixed expense is insurance. We consider it fixed because, it would be unthinkable to be on the road without insurance. Other fixed expenses will vary with each household. We have included storage because many full-timers keep a few favorite items in a storage locker someplace.

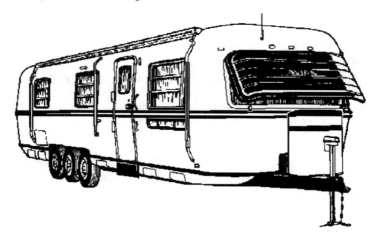

Campground Fees
Food
Fuel
Repairs
Clothing

Figure 7   Variable Expenses

This list of variable expenses (Figure 7) is common to most full-timers and some may think of others. Without experience it may be difficult to estimate these expenses accurately; however, the next chapter may be of some help. They are variable expenses because they depend on personal preferences and lifestyle. Control can be exercised over these expenditures, and the challenge will be to find ways of limiting costs that are an integral part of the full-timing operation. For example, although fuel is important, there are ways to cut back. Guidelines in Chapter 10 represent our experience.

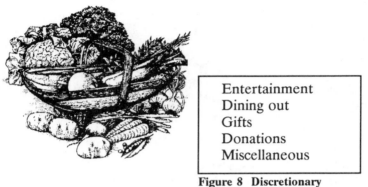

| Entertainment |
| Dining out |
| Gifts |
| Donations |
| Miscellaneous |

Figure 8 Discretionary

Discretionary expenses (Figure 8) will vary even more. Some like to dine out often, golf, or attend plays or sporting events. Special events or vacations, Super Bowl tickets, rafting trips and cruises will impact the cash planning even more. It's evident that we have more control over discretionary expense and, if need be, can eliminate them altogether in a particularly lean month.

Using the best available information and planning, a cash flow schedule may look something like this:

CASH FLOW SCHEDULE

	JANUARY	FEBRUARY	MARCH
BEG CASH BAL	$3,500.00	$3,280.00	$3,550.00
INCOME			
Interest	300.00	300.00	300.00
Social Security	680.00	680.00	680.00
Pension	800.00	800.00	800.00
TOTAL INCOME	1,780.00	1,780.00	1,780.00
EXPENSES			
Groceries	325.00	325.00	325.00
Storage	50.00	50.00	50.00
Gasoline	150.00	150.00	150.00
Gifts	50.00	20.00	30.00
Donations	50.00	40.00	50.00
RV payment	300.00	300.00	300.00
Propane	25.00	25.00	25.00
Campground fees	250.00	250.00	250.00
RV & veh repairs	100.00	100.00	100.00
Insurance	500.00	0.00	0.00
License fees	0.00	0.00	0.00
Memberships	0.00	50.00	0.00
Entertainment	100.00	100.00	100.00
Miscellaneous	100.00	100.00	100.00
TOTAL EXPENSE	2,000.00	1,510.00	1,480.00
INCOME LESS EXPENSE	(220.00)	270.00	300.00
ENDING BAL	**$3,280.00**	**$3,550.00**	**$3,850.00**

Going through this exercise, using personal experience, will provide a good handle on how income and expenditures adapt to full-timing. The schedule can be extended over a period of years, particularly if income or expenditures will change in a year or two. Personal responsibilities may decrease, or perhaps it will be helpful to recognize when social security or an annuity kicks in.

If a sound cash flow schedule has been developed, it will go a long way toward contributing to one's peace of mind as the full-timing adventure begins. If, on the other hand, the schedule comes up short, plans can be made for supplemental part-time work and/or free camping. If the schedule works out like ours, the modest financial demands of full-timing will become apparent.

♥   ♥

From The November 1992 issue of Movin' On

THE FULL-TIMER'S INVESTMENT EDGE

by Ron

Does being on the road full-time affect investment programs? This full-timer thinks it actually helps manage an effective program. Many retirees are back in the stock market because blue chip stock dividends are more attractive than CD interest rates. That is particularly true when earnings of these companies assure that the dividends will continue. If you manage your own program, you already know that your broker is only a phone call away using a toll free 800 number.

Where does the full-timer advantage come in? It is my opinion that the full-timer has a broader perspective of national business operations. As we travel we observe some consistencies in retail operations and manufactured products, both good and bad.

These observations, along with other information, help in our stock selections. We also gain insight into regional opportunities as we travel. There are many outstanding companies that operate only in a two or three state area, often overlooked by investors in other parts of the country.

Any conservative investor will look for at least three things in a company: good management, return on investment (dividends) and earnings in comparison to the price of the stock (price/earnings ratio). After all, dividends cannot continue long if the company does not earn enough to pay them.

One example of the full-timer edge: In the course of our travels, we must have visited a hundred malls. Often times we passed through a J.C. Penney store on our way into the mall. Last year, Barb seemed to be always stopping in the women's section as something would catch her eye. Now wait a minute. Penney's for women's clothes? Everyone knows it's only a place to shop for kids clothes and linens. Not anymore. Progressive management has revamped the total operation with excellent name brands and stylish offerings. The changes have been dramatic, not only in the stores, but in earnings.

This, in spite of a recession. Since we observed many Penney stores, we were quicker to notice the new trend. A November 1992 purchase at $50 a share has grown to $76 a share in less than a year for a gain of 52%. There are other examples of the full-timer edge, and we have several more that we will share later. Perhaps other full-timers reading this article will reinforce our theory with examples of their own. We would love to hear from you.

Editors Note: Penny's split two for one on May 1, 1993.

From The March 1993 Issue of Movin' On

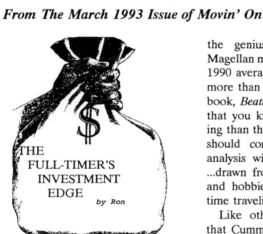

THE FULL-TIMER'S INVESTMENT EDGE
by Ron

For several months now I have been making the point that full-timers have an edge in selecting stock investments because they can recognize national marketing trends and regional booming areas as they travel. To illustrate, I mentioned several of our selections, but would like to emphasize that I do not recommend stocks. You are in a better situation to do that according to your needs and knowledge.

You may remember Peter Lynch, the genius who ran the giant Magellan mutual fund from 1977 to 1990 averaging investment gains of more than 30% a year. In his new book, *Beating the Street*, he agrees that you know more about investing than the pros. He says, "people should combine simple financial analysis with everyday knowledge ...drawn from their shopping, jobs and hobbies." We could add full-time traveling to that.

Like other full-timers, I knew that Cummings Engine just had to go up when I noticed that all the new motor homes and many pickup trucks were switching to Cummings and raving about performance. Too bad we were fully invested because that's exactly what happened.

Speaking of investments, some of our readers have unique strategies of their own. Robin Jenkinson of Bourg De Visa, France, sent me literature on South African bonds trading on the Johannesburg Stock Exchange with high yields that translate into higher profits because of currency discounts. Wow! Robin, this old accountant thought that Ford Motor was risky. On the conservative side, reader Don Laun of Modesto, California, has had success with utilities and uses their monthly dividends to supplement his retirement income. He mentions American Electric Power, San Diego Gas & Electric and Puget Power as utilities that have been good investments for him. The full-timer advantage can be used in picking utility stocks too. We couldn't help but notice that the Las Vegas area was booming and not because of gambling, but other industry. The obvious beneficiary of this growth would be Nevada Power (9% yield). Sure enough, it has risen 20% in the last 6 months. Maybe the brokerage firms should start hiring full-timers.

♥ ⌂ ♥

10

ON THE ROAD
Cost Analysis

Some may ask, "What does this perpetual vacation cost?" ...and may add, "Please be realistic, and while you're at it—be conservative." Fair enough. We can understand that, because we were also concerned as to whether or not the cash flow schedule and the carefully planned budget were realistic. So let's get down to basics.

Record Keeping

Since we began full-timing, we have kept detailed records of our expenditures, and we urge others to do the same. Our recording even included small items such as newspapers and ice cream cones. We found that after a few months of monitoring our expenditures, it was necessary to make some adjustments. At one point we analyzed our "miscellaneous" category when it seemed to be building more and more each month. By monitoring and recording miscellaneous detail for a one month period, we discovered that we needed several more expenditure categories. Some areas were large enough to accumulate expenditures by themselves.

There will be a some differences in expenditure categories among full-timers, but most will be similar. Our experience may provide an insight into the cost of full-timing. By experience, we found that we were under budgeted on several items, over on others, and right on target for most. As we examine our expenditures please note that our own biases and personal preferences affect the figures. The same will be true for you. After all, full-timers are still the same people that they were before they hit the road. It's not necessary to change unless that was in the plans when entering into retirement.

After refinement by experience, the following is how our monthly budget plan looks now. The schedule is divided into basic and discretionary expenditures along, with a minimum and maximum range, that may inspire budget tailoring after reviewing the chapter. The discussion that follows may help do that. Here then, are our expenditure guideline schedules:

BUDGET SCHEDULE

BASIC MONTHLY EXPENSE	OURS	RANGE	
		LOW	HIGH
Campground fees	$175.00	$100.00	$400.00
Fuel (both vehicles)	175.00	75.00	300.00
Groceries	350.00	200.00	500.00
Clothing	100.00	25.00	200.00
Insurance & License (2 vehicles)	125.00	50.00	300.00
Repairs & maintenance	75.00	25.00	150.00
Propane	20.00	20.00	30.00
Hospitalization & Medical	30.00	30.00	500.00
Total Basic Expense	$1,050.00	$525.00	$2,280.00

DISCRETIONARY EXPENSE

Recreation, dining out	$300.00	$50.00	$500.00
Tel answering service	20.00	0.00	30.00
Mail forwarding service	20.00	0.00	20.00
Telephone	50.00	10.00	100.00
Memberships	50.00	10.00	100.00
Storage	80.00	0.00	100.00
Gifts	50.00	0.00	100.00
Miscellaneous	75.00	50.00	100.00
Total Discretionary Expenditures	$645.00	$125.00	$1,050.00
Total Monthly Expenditures	$1,695.00	$650.00	$3,430.00

BASIC EXPENSE

As some will note, even our basic expense of $1,050, can evoke a lot of discussion, particularly the two large items—campground fees and groceries. Let us look at the items that make up our expenditure plan.

Campground Fees

If our planned figure of $175 does not fit into your income bracket, keep in mind that this is an area where many economize. There are countless ways to lower campground cost, and $175 merely represents our experience based on a combination of membership parks, commercial campgrounds, and public parks. In our first year we found that we averaged $280 per month without benefiting from campground memberships or monthly rates. We did use relatives' driveways and back yards for three or four weeks during that period along with some very reasonable state and federal parks. As we discussed in Chapter 6, many full-timers have ingenious methods of reducing or avoiding campground fees and even enjoy the camaraderie of camping with others in isolated free camping areas. In our case, we have reduced our campground cost to less than $175 through the use of a membership park system and national park volunteering.

Our campground budget figure of $175 is reasonable when considering that this includes all utilities (except propane). Many northern retirees find that their taxes and heating fuel amount to a lot more than that. Add to that, interest on the investment of a house, insurance and other related housing costs, and it's easy to see where the economies of full-timing start to materialize.

Before we leave the subject of campground expense, it's important to note that most full-timers would not be without a campground membership or two. Chapter 5 analyzes investment costs and maintenance fees of campground memberships. The costs can be prorated into a monthly figure. Like us, those using membership campgrounds, should realize a large savings, live better, and easily be within the $175 budgeted monthly.

Obviously, the lower end of our range will require a lot of boondocking, possibly some inexpensive national forest campgrounds and perhaps some campground hosting or other volunteering. At the higher end of the range, we find full-timers who own several campground memberships with their associated maintenance costs and investment. Many, at the higher range will also stay in luxurious commercial parks where 50 amp electricity is available for their large bus-type rigs and a golf course or marina might be included as additional amenities.

Gasoline

This budget item, pegged at $175, may need some adjustment depending on market conditions and individual travel approach to full-timing. During our first year of full-timing, we averaged $192 a month (pre Gulf crisis) for both motorhome and tow vehicle. In our second year we averaged $142 a month although fuel prices were higher. It's easy to explain. The first year was a time when we were really moving. Anxious to see everything, we seldom stayed at any one place more than a week, and it was not uncommon to move on after two or three days. As fuel costs increased, we realized that it was not necessary to move so often, and that longer stays would greatly reduce our fuel expense. If we stayed in an area for a month (taking advantage of a monthly rate), our fuel costs would be in the $25 range. That's all our small tow vehicle would use. We feel that even with higher fuel prices, the $175 is very realistic. In support of that we offer the following hypothetical figures. If the full-timing RV is a motorhome with a tow vehicle, and $25 is allocated to the tow vehicle for vicinity mileage, this leaves $150, which at $1.30 a gallon, will purchase approximately 115 gallons of fuel. If the RV operates at eight miles per gallon of fuel, the budget figure of $175 will still allow movement of the "home" over 900 miles every month. Longer stays and shorter moves between stays will reduce this even more. Assume the average stay is one week, and monthly fuel expense is $150 per month. If fuel increases 30% and the average stay is extended two or three days, it should be possible to stay within the planned fuel budget.

The figures will vary if living in a fifth-wheel or travel trailer. The towing vehicles necessary to tow these types of RVs are equipped with powerful engines. Those planning to tow a fifth-wheel or travel trailer may want to consider one of several diesel models on the market, which when not towing, average 20 plus miles per gallon. Fuel economy is important because the towing vehicle becomes transportation around town.

Groceries

Obviously, this is another expense that depends on individual preferences and tastes. We include in groceries, everything purchased in a grocery store. Such things as cleaning supplies, paper plates, and personal hygiene items are counted as groceries. Food preparation tends to be simple for full-timers who use microwaves, RV stoves and ovens, camp stoves and sometimes even cook over an open fire. We have found that our costs are slightly less than before full-timing, but attribute this to retirement rather than full-timing (less dependence on convenience foods). However, like other retirees, food is a major part of our budget.

On the plus side we now have more time to shop and it

does take time to take advantage of the coupons that we carefully clip. We have been introduced to new foods in different parts of the country. In Louisiana we savored red beans and rice, and we ate wonderful Mexican food in the Rio Grande Valley of Texas. We enjoyed catfish in Arkansas, fresh shrimp in South Carolina, and all types of seafood in Florida. In upper New York state, we lived on fresh produce from the roadside stands.

Besides avoiding convenience foods, our costs are slightly less because we look for local produce as we travel, and find that we are eating more vegetables and fresh fruit. That's a good idea anyway, regardless of cost. It's also a good idea to buy a local newspaper to assist in bargain shopping when in a new location.

On the negative side, we find that limited storage does not allow us to take advantage of quantity buying when items are on sale. It doesn't take long, however, to spot chain discount stores as we travel, and they always have large lots for easy parking. Even if we are not going to shop, those parking lots are a good place to stop and fix lunch.

Clothing

Clothing should not be a major part of the budget, depending on the quantity and condition of the wardrobe when taking to the road. Most retirees, whether they are full-timers or not, say that this cost decreases dramatically after retirement. Since the full-timing lifestyle is decidedly casual, jeans, shorts, tee-shirts, sweat shirts and tennis shoes will become the mainstay of the wardrobe. About the only clothing purchases we make are tennis shoes and an occasional pair of jeans or a sweat shirt. We also carry several changes of "Sunday-go-to-meeting" clothes. Variety is not necessary because we are seldom in the same place long enough to make a difference; and besides, we don't think God notices when we're wearing the same outfit in church. When we stored our extra clothes in a storage locker we used to change our wardrobe, when we returned to that area. Like so many of these categories, the wide range that is shown depends on personal preference and income. It's hard to resist the many beautiful tee shirts and sweat shirts that most resort areas seem to offer.

Insurance and Licenses

Our budgeted figure of $125 a month or $1,500 a year is based on the following costs: Good Sam (National General) Insurance $1,200—full liability & collision on 1993 motorhome and 1991 tow vehicle; emergency road service $79; license plates (both vehicles—state of Texas) $175. The liability coverage is $100,000/$300,000 with property damage at $50,000. Collision includes a $100 deductible.

We consider emergency road service essential. Coast to Coast, Good Sam and Family Motor Coach Association all sponsor services that deal with RVs. With so much depending on the use of the RV (home), it is important for full-timers to have a road service that is prepared to handle large vehicles and get those vehicles to a proper repair facility, whatever the cost. The above organizations sponsor vehicle insurance companies that know what a full-timer is and understand their particular problems. They understand that we may have a mail forwarding address in one state, while the vehicles are licensed in another state. There are several other companies that understand the full-timing concept, and it is important to deal with such a company. As our range suggests, costs will depend on the age and value of the vehicle(s), driving records, and the state where the vehicles are licensed. The higher range will reflect such states as California, Arizona and New York. We do not feel that our full-timing lifestyle has increased our insurance costs. The cost of RV insurance is usually less than that of house insurance.

Since full-timers carry expensive equipment with them such as computers, two TVs, VCRs and sports equipment, a personal contents inventory sheet will be helpful in determining if the standard contents clause in the policy should be increased. This inventory, along with serial numbers and pictures, should be duplicated and mailed to a close friend or relative for "off premises" safe keeping. Although infrequent, RV fires spread fast with little or no time to secure important papers necessary for insurance settlement.

Repairs and Maintenance

Some full-timers are mechanically inclined. If so, it will make a difference on this budget item. The age and condition of the RV and vehicle(s) will also affect repair costs. We underestimated repair and maintenance costs in our initial budget planning. Although our motorhome was only two years old, when we began full-timing, it didn't take us long to realize that motorhome mechanical repairs can be expensive when you are on the road. This was emphasized when we picked up a load of bad fuel in California, and despite repeated servicing along the way, did not get the problem resolved until our original truck dealer in Michigan came to our rescue.

Our initial tow car was at that age when the starter, alternator, battery, shocks, and carburetor all decided that they needed attention. After the clutch, and transmission went, we decided to cut our losses and purchase a new tow vehicle.

We still don't have a good handle on repairs and maintenance. Some will think $75 a month too high because they change their own oil and do their own repairs. Some months there will be no expenditures, but then the time will come to replace all the tires on our motorhome, and those big tires aren't cheap. Carefully recording all costs over a period of time will eventually provide a ball park budget figure. We continue to hope that we can live within the $75 budget now that we have a late model tow vehicle and a new motorhome. It should be easy because we also purchased an extended warranty on the motorhome.

Propane

Propane is a necessary expense for most full-timers, although it's surprising how long a tank will last. Usage will depend on whether the campsite has electricity. If not, it's necessary to use more propane for refrigeration and heating. Most RV refrigerators can now be switched to either electricity or propane. Dry camping will require more propane usage, but that will be offset by lower or nonexistent camping fees. In a moderate climate, even when dry camping, propane expenditures should not exceed $30 a month.

Hospitalization and Medical

For many this will be their biggest expense whether they are full-timers or not. We are blessed with full coverage under our retirement plan, but realize that most are not. We discuss getting medical care on the road in Chapter 11, and feel that it is not difficult to handle for most full-timers. However, the cost of such medical care is a national problem that, unfortunately, affects many retirees. Being on the road should not change these cost figures. Hopefully, less stress, more physical activity and healthier eating habits (remember the roadside vegetable stands) will reduce medical costs for most full-timers.

DISCRETIONARY EXPENSE

Recreation

For some this may be the largest item in their budget and for others it's only minimal. Personal finances, hobbies and even weather can influence the recreation budget. If the RV is parked in Las Vegas for a week, the whole month's entertainment budget could be shot. On the other hand, a week in Big Bend National Park (103 miles from the nearest shopping area) could be very economical. We include dining out in the recreation category and some may disagree with that. By dining out we mean a good evening meal served in a moderately priced (or higher) restaurant. Lunches at McDonald's, Taco Bell or Burger King are included in groceries. This works for us since we have budgeted that way.

If both full-timers are avid golfers and are spending the winter in Florida, there may be a need to increase the recreation budget. Other physical activities such as walking, hiking and biking do not affect the recreation budget except for one-time equipment purchases.

Several items that we include in the "membership" category could also be included in the recreation budget. Full-timers find that their recreation expense can be reduced by certain memberships, particularly those that are national in scope. One of these memberships is the "Golf Card" allowing free play at hundreds of golf courses around the country with only the rental of a golf cart.

Other memberships that reduce recreation costs are found in such national organizations as the Elks, Moose, Eagles, Veterans of Foreign Wars, and American Legion. These organizations often have excellent dining facilities providing reasonable meals for members. It's also a great way to meet people when in a strange town. Local members welcome visiting guests and make them feel at home.

One of our treasured friendships was made at an Elks Club in Hot Springs, Arkansas. When we explained to the waitress that we were full-timers living and traveling in a motorhome, the couple next to us, overhearing the conversation, invited us to join them at their table. Wayne and Judy Richards have been looking forward to full-timing when they retire in a few years and had lots of questions. A week later we joined them at their home for dinner and shared experiences. They also joined us for dinner several weeks later at the campground. We are now like long time friends. Speaking of Elks Clubs, we have found that many have excellent Friday night fish fries and camping spots for visiting members.

Telephone Answering Service

This is also called voice mail, and like the mail forwarding service, may be classified by some as a luxury. We discussed the pros and cons of such a service in Chapter 8. Even if we didn't think it was worth it, I'm sure our children and parents would.

Mail Forwarding Service

To some, a mail forwarding service may also be a luxury. We feel that the cost of $62 a year, plus postage, gives us a feeling of independence and assures us of professional uninterrupted mail service. Many full-timers handle mail in a less expensive way through a relative or friend.

Telephone

Full-timers have choices when it comes to telephone service. They can go to a pay phone and feed it change or use a telephone calling card. The cards cost nothing and are easy to obtain. Quite contrary to popular belief, it's not necessary to have a telephone to get a telephone calling card. We had AT&T as our long distance company when our house was on a firm foundation so requested their card. "Keeping-in-touch" telephone costs may be higher for full-timers. Calling card calls are more expensive than calls made from a home phone. But they are cheaper than collect or third party calls. AT&T explained that all calling card calls are billed at cost plus 80 cents. Collect calls are cost plus $1.75 or $2.50. We feel that our newsletter, short notes and postcards help reduce this cost. Although we may have a few more long distance calls to pay for, we do not have to pay a basic monthly telephone rate which can amount to $20 or more. The alternative to a telephone calling card is a pocket full of loose change.

Memberships

We have already mentioned the Golf Card and fraternal organizations. For full-timers this budget item can be substantial, but cost effective. Some of our cost-effective memberships are the Good Sam Club, Kampgrounds of America (KOA), Coast to Coast, Escapees, and Family Motor Coach Association. Others may be added to this list. Everyone's list should include membership in the Good Sam Club. The nominal cost provides a 10% discount on campgrounds, propane and RV supplies.

Storage

This is probably a luxury (some might even call it a security blanket) costing $80 a month for a 10' x 20' space. We are presently in the process of discontinuing our storage arrangement. Most people will feel the need to store treasured personal items, favorite pictures, electronic equipment and other items that will be expensive to replace if the time comes to settle down. It may be possible, however, to reduce the number of stored items and provide for less expensive storage at a son or daughter's home. Perhaps a little storage shed in back of their garage will suffice. There has to be a better way than paying $960 a year to store $3,000 worth of possessions. During the first year of full-timing it may be worthwhile to have such a security blanket, but as full-timing stretches into years, reevaluation is necessary.

Gifts, Donations, Church Contributions, Etc.

This is a highly personal area for all of us. Unfortunately, many of us cannot maintain our pre-retirement levels of giving. We try to find inexpensive, yet unique, gifts that represent the area of the country we are currently in. Our grown children are so hard to buy for. Christmas 1991, we made up a box of goodies for each of our children, containing a product from each of the northwestern states we had just visited. Such items as huckleberry jelly from Montana, mustard from Oregon, BBQ sauce from Idaho, home made jelly from Utah, and bread mix from Washington, made up the gift boxes. It was a great idea and the expense was spread out over five months, but it was difficult to store nine of everything (one for each of our children) in our little house. The expense of mailing made these gifts expensive, so now we will just shop for the grandchildren. We like to send little things all year-long—even if it is just post cards and stickers. Children love mail. By the way, US Savings Bonds make nice birthday gifts for grandchildren.

Contributions need not always be in the form of money either. Volunteer activities can take many directions and will be appreciated by charitable organizations. Retirees can do things for free that an organization would otherwise have to pay for. Another idea is to redirect gifts. It's no secret that full-timers are very hard to buy for. They do not have much room for "things" and have few needs. We suggested that a gift be given in our names to a favorite charity and even named a few. Our children were relieved to hear of the plan. They can even take a tax deduction. Everyone gains.

Miscellaneous

Many of the items found charged to miscellaneous are really basic to full-timing. Some may want to provide separate categories for them. Most full-timers frequent laundromats once a week. Our laundry costs average five dollars a week and we charge that to miscellaneous. Other items include postage, books, computer supplies, newspapers and magazines.

In this chapter we have discussed costs on the road as we have found them. Using our experience as a base may be helpful in planning. A budget is a spending *plan* and as such, needs to be evaluated and revised constantly. The bottom line will need to coincide with planned incomes, but there can be tradeoffs along with innovative solutions to budget problems. As in solving most problems, discussion is important. When both partners are involved in the preparation process and monthly review (important), a good product evolves and commitment is not a problem. Anyway—full-timers are used to doing things together.

♥ ♥

From the April 1991 issue of Movin' On

A CHANGE OF LIFESTYLE
Campground Hosting in Yosemite

As I sit here typing this I am aware of the sound of the Merced River nearby—I can see the white water from my window here in the Wawona Campground. Our house sets just a chip shot (90 feet) from the river. It is quiet here except for the water and the birds; occasionally I hear the breeze rustling the leaves; once in a while I hear a deer searching for tender foliage just across the road in the woods.

Even when the campground is busy, it is a quiet campground. People seem to sense the peacefulness here and keep it that way. At night I can look around and see lots of campfires, but all I hear is the crackle of the logs burning.

This is truly different from the Coast to Coast campgrounds and their club houses, swimming pools and tennis courts. There we would have electricity. Here we don't.

When we arrived on April 1, we were relieved to find that we had water and sewer hookups because our ranger boss, Kevin, had mentioned the day before that we didn't. We really didn't think we could stay under those conditions since there are no showers, and it was one mile to a dump station. We were so happy when the first thing

Kevin said was, "I made a mistake, you do have water and sewer." We were getting settled at the campsite and wondered aloud where the electrical hookup was. Kevin answered, "There is no electricity anywhere in the campground." We said, "April fool" (remember, it was April 1) and he said, "No, I wouldn't kid you." We discussed the situation and thought we could make it, especially, since we had our little 600-watt generator and they promised to give us lots of firewood.

It gets mighty cold here in the evening and not a lot warmer during the day. The first three weeks, we saw night time temperatures in the mid-twenties.

At first, we ran our furnace enough to be comfortable and quickly ran our battery down. Ron tried running the generator during the day to charge it up, but we were losing ground. We made the decision to use the furnace only in the morning to take the chill off.

We build a fire at night and stay by it until 10 o'clock when we come in, light a candle (for warmth), climb on the bed with our clothes on, cover up with the afghan, turn on the light over the bed and read until the cold gets unbearable, about 30 minutes. By then, the bed has been warmed and we undress and climb under the covers. Our duvet (down comforter) is so nice and warm that once under the covers we are toasty. Only our faces get cold by morning. In fact, it gets so cold in our house at night that ice left in a glass of water at night is still there in the morning.

Before we get out of bed I turn on the furnace (the thermostat is right on the wall next to my side of the bed) and wait for the indoor temperature to get to at least 40^0 before I get up to make coffee. Since we use the gas stove to make coffee, that helps warm us too. Once the coffee is done, we go outside and build a fire again to keep warm.

We had to have son Karl get our "long johns" out of storage and send them to us; and we always wear several layers of clothing. I am so glad we had winter coats, hats and gloves with us too. We have made a game out of keeping warm.

But we get to take brisk walks in the morning (that is always good for warming one up) and breathe lots of fresh air. We watch the coyotes, and the deer watch us. We spend hours searching the woods for firewood and meet lots of wonderful people (and a few not so nice ones). The rangers, as usual, are super and can't do enough for us and in return, we try to do a good job for them.

So, if you are wondering why your newsletter is late, it is because I hate to ruin the quiet here by running the generator (I need it for the printer and to recharge the computer) and I'd rather be wandering in the woods, by the fire where it is warm, or talking to our campers. Sorry about that!!! Bear with us for one more month while we struggle without electricity.

Editors note: They don't usually use campground hosts in the Wawona Campground until mid-May. We were an experiment. When we arrived, there was 4-feet of snow on the ground. It was a great experience.

From The April 1991 Issue of Movin' On

POTPOURRI
By Ron

* Do you know what a bear box is? Every campsite here at the Wawona Campground has one. It's a long metal box where campers protect their food from the bears. If you leave food unattended in this campground, you may be fined. Yogi has to find his own food in the woods.

* Speaking of bears, Ranger Kevin McMillan in his talk on bear encounters gives tips on storing food while backpacking. He also says that when hiking in bear country it is best to go with someone who runs slower than yourself.

* The river that runs next to this campground is so cold that even the fish pass it up. It looks like a beautiful northern Michigan trout stream with rushing water over the rocks, but no one has caught a fish yet.

* Our Plymouth Horizon tow car is showing it's age. This month it needed a new clutch and a catalytic converter. Luckily we found an excellent repair shop in Oakhurst, 25 miles from here.

* I like the "host" part of our campground hosting job, such as helping campers with site selection and information. I don't care much for the "policing" activities that are too often necessary.

* I still look at the sports page every day, but only to keep track of how many games Jack Morris (spoiled millionaire formerly with the Tigers and now with the Twins) has lost.

* You should see my partner in her new ranger-type uniform. Very sharp!

♥ △ ♥

11

ON THE ROAD
Special Considerations

When we are parked in a winter resort, we are often asked where home is. We answer that home is where we park it. We think that is cute, and it really is true. That answer, however, is not good enough for the tax collector and most insurance companies. Although we won't be "living" there, it is necessary to establish a home base for taxes, insurance, licenses, and voting. Some may think of other reasons.

Selecting A Home Base

Most full-timers take great care in selecting a home base, and taxes play a large part in that decision. All states have residency requirements, and research may be necessary to insure compliance. Generally, there are ways to comply and still maintain a roving lifestyle without an investment in property. It may involve more than just establishing a mail forwarding address there. On the other hand, using a relative's address may be sufficient. Publications are available listing tax and licensing requirements in each state. One such publication is *Drivers License Administration Requirements and Fees* and can be ordered free from The Federal Highway Administration, Department of Transportation, 400 7th St. S.W., Room 4208, Washington, D.C. 20590.

A low personal income tax state may have high licensing fees and sales tax. When considering that an 8% sales tax on a new RV in the $50,000 range will cost $4,000, sales tax becomes a major factor. After several years on the road, we have selected Texas as our home base. Although the sales tax is 6.25% on new vehicles, they only tax on the difference between the new vehicle and the trade-in. There is no state income tax and vehicle license fees are very reasonable. During our second year of full-timing, we moved our mail forwarding service to Texas, so the change was a natural. It helps that we like Texas and spend a lot of time there. We actually feel like Texans, although, we haven't acquired the Texas drawl . . . yet.

Licenses

Normally vehicle tags are not difficult to obtain when on the road. In most states this can be accomplished through the mail. For new vehicles it will take some planning to insure that insurance documentation, titles, weight slips and other necessary paperwork are completed before mailing in the application. If the mail process will delay getting the information, perhaps a relative or friend, living in the resident state, will personally handle the transaction using an overnight mail service to receive paperwork and return license tags. Normally, there is sufficient time, because all states issue temporary licenses at a nominal charge for new vehicles. Existing vehicles can be handled easier with preprinted application forms automatically mailed out by the issuing state.

Driver's licenses are another matter. The bad news is that it may be necessary to appear in person. Some states have a mail process; however, they often require periodic personal appearances. The good news is that driver's licenses are often good for four years. It will be necessary to plan around these renewal dates and schedule itineraries accordingly. When the licensing state is the original home territory, family visits and reunions can coincide with the renewal. If it is not possible to return to the issuing state at the time of renewal, many states will issue a temporary or even a permanent license. The important thing is to have a valid license in your possession, regardless of issuing state.

Insurance

Insurance, of course, can be handled by mail. As noted in Chapter 10, insurance companies are not used to dealing with full-timers and may not understand the situation. When not comfortable with a company's reaction and solutions to full-timing, consider talking to one of the several companies that advertise in RV magazines. They specialize in RV insurance and understand the circumstances and needs of full-timers.

The selection of a home base will also affect RV insurance. Since state laws vary, this becomes important. The home base address affects rates because insurance companies rate according to geographic location within a state. The most important rating factor, however is driving record. Residence or place registered, will make little difference when a poor driving record influences the insurance application.

Voting

The obvious solution to voting is the absentee ballot and it's not easy. It's against the law for city or county clerks to mail an absentee ballot automatically. It will require a separate request for each election. The request should be made at least two months before the election in order to allow plenty of time for delays due to mail forwarding and for responding. It will be difficult to keep up with the local issues and candidates. We have found that it is sometimes necessary to bypass a particular race or proposition when we have no background. Some may have ways of keeping on top of the local issues, particularly, when planning to return and live in the area some day. The whole process of voting and using an address where one does not reside is shaky at best. Election laws do not take full-timers into consideration. The whole issue needs to be addressed. Perhaps in the future, organizations like Good Sam, or Escapees will discuss this at the national level.

Census

We pay our taxes, vote and consider ourselves good citizens. Therefore, we were upset when it became obvious that we would not be counted in the 1990 census. Since we are part of a large community of full-timers, we wrote to the U.S. Census Bureau Headquarters in Denver, expressing dismay that a large segment of the population was slipping through the cracks. We explained that we were just as important as the homeless in the New York subways that they had taken great measures to count. We are not homeless—our homes just move. Their response was to send a census form to our mail forwarding service. The form letter said not to mail it—they would pick it up. We wonder if they are still looking for us? Just for the record, we did mail it back to them.

As the number of full-timers grows, we hope that our

government will recognize us and make it easier for full-timers to handle these problems. We should have a represent-ative at large, an United States drivers license and voting privileges in, at least, the national elections. And while they're at it, how about a national fishing license. Perhaps an organi-zation like the American Association of Retired Persons (AARP) will carry the ball on this.

Medical

Medical considerations deter many people from becoming full-timers and often for good reason. If either spouse re-quires specialized medical attention frequently, full-timing can present some problems. This is particularly true if one is comfortable only with a family doctor or specialist. There is nothing wrong with that. Full-timing, as we describe it, may not be for those people. On the other hand, we know two who have not let their health problems stop them. Joycene has severe arthritis and takes gold shots regularly. To do this she must visit a doctor, get blood tests after which she gets the shot. She does not consider her condition a deterrent to the lifestyle. We met a campground host couple at Gulf Islands National Seashore near Pensicola, Florida. She was on oxygen 24-hours a day through a permanent endo-tracheal tube. Although they had to work around getting oxygen in any state, they say it has not kept them from enjoying the full-timing lifestyle.

Others, with ailments or conditions that require only an annual or semi-annual checkup, probably can handle dealing with a new doctor and different medical facilities. Ron fits into this latter category. A 1986 heart attack still requires annual checkups and a review of medications being taken. This has not been a problem. Stress tests and cardiograms are the same in Texas or Arizona as they are in Michigan. It is essential, no matter which state the doctor is in, that his or her orders be followed. It is also vital to carry medical records on the road. They are easy to get, and every doctor is required to provide a copy when requested by the patient. Besides saving time and expense, they are very helpful to a physician not familiar with a patient's case history.

When we find that it is time for checkups or eye examinations, we look for a city with a population of about 20,000, and include it in our travel schedule. A city of this size will usually have complete medical facilities, but is small enough to provide personalized attention. We were extremely pleased with the treatment we received in Bend, Oregon, and the effort made by those physicians to schedule needed tests in a short period of time. Because of their thorough efforts, Barb's asthma condition was diagnosed and properly treated so that our full-timing could continue uninterrupted. We also obtained appointments for eye examinations, and received our new glasses in just a few days. Our 10 day visit to Bend took care of our medical needs in a prompt, professional manner, allowing time for sight seeing and some of the best pizza we have ever eaten.

In recent years a proliferation of emergency outpatient clinics and sports medicine clinics has occurred around the country. These clinics can be helpful to full-timers and provide a solution to the problem of finding a doctor. Costs are usually reasonable and can be charged to a credit card. Some will even bill the health care provider direct. We used a sports medicine clinic in San Antonio when an earlier bicycle fall continued to cause a nagging sore shoulder. An appointment was made for that afternoon and the treatment was thorough including X-rays (negative) and directions for muscle exercises.

Obtaining medicine is now easier in the computer age. Many chain pharmacies can pull a prescription out of the system, even though the original may be several states away. We are fortunate that our health care provider participates in a mail order system that keeps our prescriptions on file and mails our prescriptions when requested by us. Many companies are now doing this. The American Association of Retired Persons (AARP) also advertises a prescription mail order service. Our mail order prescription service is handled by *Caremark,* 625 Barclay Boulevard, Lincolnshire, Illinois, 60069. We noticed, while staying along the Mexican border, that many full-timers were crossing the border to purchase prescription and non-prescription drugs at a fraction of the normal cost.

For many, dental care can be a problem when it comes to major work. Family dentists over the years know every filling and bridge that we have in our mouths. However, their records are as easy to come by as medical records and will assist in getting good dental care on the road. Have your dentist make any special notes that would help the new dentist. But some of us are more picky about a dentist then we are about a doctor. Generally this does not include the dental hygienist, so there is no reason to avoid an annual or semiannual teeth cleaning. Except for emergency work, we plan to delay major dental work (when needed) to the time when our schedule takes us back to our long time family dentist. So far—so good.

Weddings, and Other Special Occasions

Who wouldn't want to be with family and friends on special occasions? Admittedly, there have been some that we have missed and that's the downside of our chosen lifestyle.

Except for funerals and serious illnesses, most family gatherings are planned months in advance. There are three courses of action that we can take with the planned events. One, we can elect not to attend if distance and schedule become a problem. Two, we can plan our travel itinerary to coincide with the event. Three, we can use our tow vehicle or commercial transportation to travel the distance, leaving our motorhome where it is, and saving the expense of moving it long distances.

We have used all three methods. We were in southwestern Texas when we got a message on our voice mail that son Mark, in California, was getting married in just one month. We had not planned on traveling any further west than New Mexico, but changed our plans and traveled the extra distance to be a part of the wedding. Sadly, we have missed several family weddings because of volunteering commitments or distance.

When daughter, Susie, announced her December wedding in July, we could plan effectively. Since we had planned on being in the southwest that winter, we picked a spot slightly southwest to spend October and November. It had to be fairly warm because cold weather and RVs don't mix. Also, we didn't want to be too far away so that we could easily drive our little tow vehicle back to Michigan. We then plotted on a map an area 700 to 900 miles south and slightly west of Lansing, Michigan. That area covered several national parks, Corps of Engineer camping sites and many state parks. We picked out four and sent applications for volunteer work to The Great Smoky Mountains National Park, Hot Springs National Park and two Corps of Engineer sites. Our applications included our work experience and stated that we would be available during the months of October and November. We received responses from all four parks including several telephone calls on our voice mail service. We selected the first to respond. The result was a two-month volunteer commitment at Hot Springs National Park in Arkansas. This delightful assignment placed us 900 miles from Michigan and was a perfect jumping off point for Texas and points further west after the wedding. Luckily, many other weddings and graduations are held in June, a good time to spend a month or two in Michigan.

Repairs

Just like the permanent home, the RV home will sometimes require repairs or alterations. In the case of a motorhome, problems with any part of the unit will require taking the home along to the repair facility. We have experienced this lately due to warranty work done on our motorhome. Any new RV will have to have some warranty work done, the same as a house. In our case, we spent a total of seven days at LazyDays RV Center in Tampa, Florida, when we bought the motorhome. It took three days to move in, and we came back a week later for minor repairs. At Ancira RV and GM in Boerne, Texas, we spent a total of six days getting more warranty work done. Both experiences were excellent. RV dealerships understand the full-timing concept and go out of their way to make the full-timer comfortable. At LazyDays, they provided a comfortable lounge complete with comfortable furnishings, TV and fresh coffee. At both places, those having repairs done, were taken to lunch each day.

RV dealers know that full-timers may be far away from their original selling dealer and accept the fact that they will do warranty work on units that they did not sell. Likewise, other dealers may be performing warranty work on units that they sold. They understand that full-timers live in their units and provide facilities accordingly. Many have areas with hookups for overnight stays. Those that don't will simply run an electrical cord to the unit while it is parked outside the service bay overnight. Security is no problem, because all dealers secure their own facility at night. It may take several days in a service facility to complete the repair, especially when special parts need to be ordered. Whether it's warranty work or other repairs, we would feel comfortable spending that time at a dealership. During the day it's fun to look at the new models on display and to explore the surrounding areas in our little tow car.

Repair work on the road can be a scary proposition. We

have all heard horror stories about fake repairs, rip-offs and shoddy work. Further, when traveling, it is not always possible to return to the scene of the crime when work proves to be faulty. Because of this, we deal primarily with national companies having organizations in every state. Even though their dealerships are privately owned, they can exert a lot of pressure to get things right.

Single Full-Timers

We really hadn't been paying much attention to the fact that there are a lot of single full-timers out there. After the first edition of this book, we received a lot of mail from singles contemplating the full-timing lifestyle. They liked the idea, but wondered if there were other singles living full-time in an RV. If so, what problems were they encountering? Thinking back, we remembered that we had met some single people on the road, but had failed to include this facet in the book.

We can remember meeting, on five different occasions, single women full-timers. Two were traveling in conversion vans. We met Nancy at Brimely State Park in Michigan's Upper Peninsula, where she was parked next to us. We met her again at Hot Springs National Park in Arkansas. The other lady traveling and living in a conversion van was visiting Arches National Park in Moab, Utah. She had just returned from a two-year stint in the Peace Corps and joined us on a strenuous ranger led hike. On an evening walk at Columbia River Gorge Coast to Coast Campground in Oregon, we met another lady full-timing in a small pickup camper. She was very enthusiastic about her lifestyle. While staying at Catalina Spa and RV Resort (CCC) in Desert Hot Springs, California, we observed another single lady full-timing in a class C motorhome with a thriving hair cutting business. A small sign in the window of the RV, and a notice on the bulletin board, brought in a lot of business. The barbering was done outside in the delightful California weather. While walking one evening at Fiesta Resorts Travel Village (CCC) near Valencia, California, we heard a voice call down to us from the roof of a 30-foot class A motorhome. The lady on the roof was repairing a broken TV antenna and wanted us to keep the shaft from turning in the coach. We were glad to help and enjoyed visiting with her. She explained that she was a single full-timer and published a newsletter called the *Silver Thread* that dealt with psychic growth. Part of her RV had been converted into an office, which she proudly showed us. She had removed one of the twin beds and replaced it with a computer desk.

We met Frank Herrington at Pedernales Hills Resort (CCC) in Johnson City, Texas. Since this friendly 71 year old man had been traveling alone for over two years, we asked him for some tips to single full-timers. After his enthusiastic endorsement of single full-timing, he offered some good suggestions. First of all, he recommended that a list of emergency contacts (names, addresses and phone numbers), along with medical information, be posted prominently in the RV. In case of a serious illness or accident, no partner is available to provide that information. He always lets campground security know that he is traveling alone and where a key to his unit will be. If he is not out and about he would like for someone to check on him. For motorhome owners Frank suggests that single full-timers invest in an adjustable or telescoping tow bar for their tow vehicle. This will help in hooking the two vehicles up alone. Frank always has a couple of extra chairs setting out under his awning as an inviting welcome. This encourages fellow campers to sit and talk for awhile. He never lacks for company and since fellow campers are always outside, he makes a point of stopping for chats when he takes his nightly bike ride around the campground. Frank says, "A man traveling by himself has flat got it made." He went on to explain that couples are always inviting him over for dinner. Last summer he traveled to Alaska for three months and had a ball. While en route, he met up with a group of other RVers and joined them for the rest of the trip.

Frank also thought that subscribing to one of the medical air services was essential for single full-timers. He felt very good about having it on his trip to Alaska. If he got sick or even broke a leg, this service would see to it that he and his motorhome got "home." Those of us with spouses should probably have this service also. We suggest MASA (Medical Air Services Association) and feel that it is not expensive at about $125 per year—not when one considers the peace of mind it offers.

There are several support groups for single full-timers and their addresses are listed in the back of this book. All of them publish newsletters, and their members network through rallies and special events. Organizations that we are aware of are: RVing Women (close to 3,000 members), Loners of America, Inc., and Loners on Wheels.

Pets On The Road

We have met many full-timers who have pets. In most cases, they wouldn't think of traveling without the family pet that had been a part of the family for many years. Pets on the road can present problems, but resourceful full-timers manage these. Some campgrounds have a "no pets" policy, but most accept them with strict guidelines. Anyone with camping experience is familiar with the six-foot leash requirement and the "pickup after your pet" policy. Several state parks do not allow pets and several others have special pet sections. To many, the inconvenience of having a pet in the full-timing household is well worth it, and they are prepared to deal with it. For some, a pet may restrict sightseeing activities. To include a pet is a personal decision.

Security

In over four years of full-timing we have never felt insecure in a camping situation. This is probably because we usually stay in campgrounds and public parks that have security. Membership campgrounds are noted for their good security and take pride in keeping nonmembers out. In a boondocking situation, the full-timer will most likely be in an unsecured area. At those times, many elect to camp with other boondockers—sort of a "circle the wagons" maneuver. No matter where one is parked, it is just good common sense to secure the RV, if only for a trip to the trash container. Such things as RV alarm systems and weapons depend on personal convictions. Generally, we are the same people that we were before full-timing. If weapons and alarms made sense to one then, a person's feelings about them will remain the same when becoming a full-timer. Personal security is a concern for many people, not just full-timers. It is our opinion that full-timing does not add to, or diminish the need for security precautions.

Dealing With Special Situations

In previous chapters, we wrote about unexpected situations being adventures. Of all the people we know, full-timers are the most adventurous. After all, they chose to be different and adopted this unusual lifestyle. They are also innovative people, and we think they can add to some of our ideas and effectively deal with life's challenges as they occur. Full-timing does not really complicate these situations once they are logically and promptly dealt with.

♥   ♥

From the September 1991 issue of Movin' On

IT'S A MATTER OF ATTITUDE

When it rains do you pout and scream or do you snuggle up in a bunch of pillows and read a book? It's that old question—is half a glass of water half full or half empty? It's simply a matter of attitude.

When many people find out that we are full-timers, they first ask how we get our mail or how we keep in touch with family and friends. That problem isn't nearly as complicated as most assume so then they go on to question other aspects of our life. What do you do about church, doctors, banking, etc? The list is endless. Recently I was asked what we would do if we were faced with a serious medical problem that required extensive treatment somewhere. I surprised myself with the answer.

If Ron or I had to be treated for something like cancer, I would ask where in the whole United States the best treatment center is and go there. Most have places to park RVs right near the facility. And if we decided to go to yet another one (no matter where), we would take off. We can go from Maine to California in a short time and stay as long as we need to. So you see this lifestyle has an advantage if you have the right attitude.

Because the Labor Day holiday was approaching, we decided to stay out of the mainstream tourist areas and get some things done. I needed a physical, and we needed to get our eyes examined, and so on. As soon as we arrived in La Pine (just 20 miles south of Bend) [Oregon], I checked out the "Physicians" section of the phone book and noticed that the Bend Memorial Clinic had a satellite clinic in La Pine. I called (it was a Wednesday) and got an appointment with Dr. Laurie Ponte on Thursday. Although they knew of our lifestyle, I was treated like I was a long time patient.

Proving what a small world it is, when I gave Dr. Ponte my medical records from MSU, she said "I graduated from MSU." One thing led to another and I discovered that she is from Ypsilanti, Michigan and actually attended both rival schools—U of M and MSU. But the important thing is, she took a real interest in my physical being and asked if I'd be willing to have a pulmonary function test and see a pulmonologist for my breathing problems. Knowing that we were going to be here only a short time, Linda (the nurse) set up all appointments in the next few days. Wherever I went, doctors and technicians went out of their way to squeeze me in, but at no time did I ever feel that I had been crowded in. I was always given all the time I needed for the exam or whatever. I just couldn't get over the care and attention I was given and they know I won't be in their care again.

I have never worried about getting health care, and this experience proves my theory. Quite frankly, I finally got some relief from a problem that has plagued me from way back before we went on the road. A forced second opinion didn't hurt—in fact, it helped.

There is a way to handle every aspect of our lifestyle, but if it is looked upon as a hassle, then it will be unbearable. Every time we come to a new town we get a thrill at the prospect of making new acquaintances. There is always a new map to study and new stores to visit. Each grocery store is a fun experience. We make a game out of finding the items we are looking for. I can't tell you in how many different sections we have found powdered milk. We know that we are going to get lost in every new town and grocery store. We laugh about it and cheer when we don't. We ask questions of clerks (where is this street or that store) and sometimes meet new friends in doing so.

You know how we get our mail, but you may not realize that mail is more exciting now than it was when we were in Haslett. We received few letters then. Now we get lots of letters from our good friends, and when it comes in a bunch once a week, it is like Christmas for us. We sit and savor each and every letter, and we don't have to deal with the junk mail. Life can be an adventure or a nightmare. It is simply a matter of attitude.

From the May 1991 Issue of Movin' On

MIRACLES DO HAPPEN

Jim and Pam arrived at the Wawona Campground one Friday night when the campground was filling up fast. It was dark out, and Barb didn't notice until morning that their license plate was from Michigan. Barb and Ron like to talk to everyone, but someone from Michigan is even more special. These partners-in-life were even more special than could have been imagined.

Jim, 34 from Detroit, and Pam 29 from Pickney, had been living full-time in their 21-foot Shasta trailer since August 1990. But their story really starts in January of 1987 when they met at Henry Ford Community College. They were lab partners in an electronics class. Jim said they were "joined electrically." Gradually their relationship. changed. What started casually evolved to love by fall of 1987. They found they had lots in common, like love of the out-of-doors and spent many weekends camping in Michigan. The early spring in 1988 was special because they spent a lot of time in Michigan woods hunting for morel mushrooms, something they both enjoyed. They both graduated in May and their future looked bright.

One morning, in July of 1988 while Pam was at work, she saw stars. She went to the rest room, and was shocked to see that she was pure white. She went out to her car, turned on the air conditioner full blast and passed out. Some construction workers found her and called an ambulance. She arrived at Providence Hospital by 10 a.m. and was in surgery by 1 p.m.. They discovered that a tumor had ruptured. It ruptured with such force that it blew open her colon, and she had been hemorrhaging. The tumor was cancerous and in rupturing had flooded her insides with cancer cells. Although the doctors felt they had gotten most of the cancer, they were not sure.

Pam said that it was so depressing at home with everyone believing she was going to die that she had to get away. Two weeks after surgery, Jim took her to Michigan's upper peninsula. They bought a canoe and just enjoyed the peace and quiet. Pam found that she could sleep comfortably in a hammock although she had to contend with the raccoons in the tree branches up above.

After two treatments of chemo, they discovered another tumor. Doctors at the University of Michigan Hospital removed the new tumor but gave her only six weeks to live. More chemo was started, and at the end of one year she was still alive and free of tumors. Everything looked good. She said that, worse than the chemo therapy was the fact that all of her long blonde hair fell out.

Three months later (Jan'90), she noticed small tumors just under her incision and was started on chemo again. After five months of treatment, the doctors said that it was hopeless. The tumors were inoperable, and chemo wasn't working. Pam wanted to go West so they both quit working, bought the used trailer, put a cap on the pickup truck as well as a rack for the canoe. Pam made a will, and said "goodby" to her family because she felt that she would never see them again. With their small savings, they took off. She said, "I felt that I had to go to a mountain and get up high, to ask God to heal me. I tried to absorb everything and Jim was so positive with me all the time." Jim had learned the value of positive thinking and imaging when he had been diagnosed as having Multiple Sclerosis. One day he woke up feeling normal and hasn't had a symptom since.

For Pam, the traveling was difficult. She was uncomfortable as the grape size tumors grew to grapefruit, orange and golf ball size. She was in constant pain and stopped, as needed, at hospitals to get pain medication.

When she stopped at Stanford University Hospital in California, the doctors were fascinated and felt they could help. Pam was full of

hope and decided to give them a try. The chemo they tried was experimental and was a disaster for Pam. She had horrible reactions—even became psychotic, but they wanted to give her one more treatment in spite of the reactions. She was one week from her next treatment, and it was the day before Thanksgiving, when the big tumor burst through the skin. Jim took Pam to Stanford where they just gave her dressings to keep the area clean, and told her to come back for her scheduled appointment. Jim drove to Yosemite, rented a wheelchair and pushed Pam all around the valley. She spent the time crying.

At her regular appointment, the doctors decided on no more chemo and suggested surgery. Because these tumors had grown, removing them would leave gaping holes in her abdomen so the suggested surgery would include a muscle graft from her back, connecting blood vessels, etc. She was in surgery for 13 hours, but Jim said that when she came out of surgery, she looked better than ever before. She was full of spirit and was released from the hospital in 10 days. She had to endure radiation therapy every day for nine weeks and is now free of any signs of cancer. She was written up in the Medical Journals and Stanford called her case the "most interesting of the year."

Barb was impressed at the hiking they did, and how alive and positive this couple was. Jim and Pam are thinking of going back to Michigan and back to work now that Pam is sure she will live. But they want to keep on camping and might settle for half time. If you see this neat looking couple, traveling in a 21' Shasta trailer pulled by a red pick up truck with a canoe on top, stop and say "hello" to them for us.

Eclipse (their dog) takes after his masters. He drags his rope through the campfire—it burns and he is free.

The next two articles are from the October 1991 issue.

POTPOURRI
By Ron

* You have to pay before pumping gas in California, while in Oregon (by law) all gasoline is pumped by an attendant. Does that tell you something about these two states?

* I thought that we were hot stuff pulling our new pickup until I saw a motorhome on I-90 pulling a trailer with a helicopter on it. I'm not kidding.

* After paying $24 (including Good Sam discount) for a campsite in Jackson, Wyoming, I really appreciate our CCC membership.

* Yellowstone brought back some not so good memories of Yosemite. Too many people (even at this time of year) and inconsiderate drivers who are always in a hurry, or stop in the middle of the road with no notice, to look at wildlife.

* I surely don't like the football scores coming out of E. Lansing. Is it time for a new coach or . . . smarter players?

* With all of the recent baby news coming our way, it sure was comforting to have our answering service. It worked great. Reminder to family: We check the service every night between 7 and 9 p.m., E.S.T.

* Barb talked me into buying a leather "Indiana Jones" hat in Idaho. Maybe we will show you a picture of me wearing it in the next issue.

* My favorite park this past month was Mt. Rainier—unique and beautiful!

THIS N
THAT

by
    Barbara

It was dusk at the Columbia River Gorge campground (Oregon) and I wanted to get a better view of the upcoming sunset. I grabbed Ron and we started to walk to a good spot when out of the corner of my eye I spotted a snake. I just knew it was a rattler. Of course I did the only respectable thing —screamed, and practically broke Ron's arm dragging us away. We watched the snake slither away but all the while I was shaking. Ron calmly assured me that it was no rattler but that didn't matter, I went back inside and let the sun set by itself. In fact I vowed that I would not venture out at night even if our house was on fire. The next day at church, we were talking to some folks and they asked where we were staying. Ron told him and the man responded with, "Oh, up there with all the rattlesnakes." I'll never believe Ron again.

Washington State has some interesting names of towns and cities. How would you pronounce Snoqualmie? How about Puyallup? Leave out the "l" in Snoqualmie and you'll say it right (snow-qua-me). Pew -all-up is the other one, and once you have a good teacher it is easy. Thanks Carol Anne.

Do you remember the article about my reunion with my best friend from my Air Force days (Feb-91)? I didn't mention it at the time, but Glenda is being treated for lung cancer in Houston and is struggling. Can I ask any of you who will to include her in your prayers? Although she has traveled the world, she has missed seeing the United States in depth, and I want her to be able to do that soon. Thanks

I goofed in the last newsletter and had a typo in the quiz. The tallest tree in the world is 367 feet not 376. That is roughly as tall as a 37-story building and is in Redwood National Park.

I am really lucky that one of my kids travels as much as he does. Robert has visited us at more campgrounds than any of our kids. He gets a big kick out of finding us "at home" wherever he goes. I am not going to Alaska in the Winter though. No thank you.

I can't tell you how much I love the West, and if I had my whole life to live over that is where I would live. Every time I think I have found heaven on earth I go a little further down the road and find "another heaven." Gosh, this country is beautiful especially the mountainous west. Part of the secret is traveling the little back roads. I started writing the VGGG (Volcanos, Ghosts, Glaciers and Geysers) article by describing all the little state and U.S. routes we took, but it made the article too long and I had to cut it all out.

Here is a quote from Mary Walker's journal which was written in the 1840's. She was one of those rugged western pioneers:
"Rose about five. Had breakfast. Got my housework done about nine. Baked six loaves of bread.

Made a kettle of mush and now a suet pudding and beef boiling. I have managed to put my clothes away and set my house in order. May the merciful be with me through the unexpected scene ...Nine o'clock p.m. was delivered of another son."
I'll remember this anytime I think I have had a bad day.

I have picked up a couple of books about women who toured the West in the late 1800's and early 1900's. These are wealthy women who could afford the trip, but they didn't sit in some automobile to tour. Can you imagine climbing to Half Dome, or Mt. Rainier in long skirts, etc.? They did!! I really wanted to hike to a glacier at Rainier, but I had an excuse. I had broken my little toe the day before we left Bend. If those ladies could do it in long skirts and slippery shoes, I should have gone on with my broken toe.

♥ ⌂ ♥

Ron And Barb At Work At Home
Going For A Bike Ride
At Home At The LBJ Ranch, Texas

—1993 Austin American-Statesman Photos By Rebecca McEntee

12

ON THE ROAD
Good And Bad Times

Prior to this chapter, we have discussed many of the logistical, technical and financial problems of the full-timer. So by now, potential full-timers don't expect to enter a trouble-free land of enchantment. They may escape their troublesome brother-in-law, but everyday life still has the concerns, troubles, and nuisances that existed before hitting the road. True, the surroundings will be new and the problems may even be different, but there will be problems. In other words, **the full-timing lifestyle is not an escape.** We take our hang ups, abilities, habits, likes, dislikes, prejudices, and opinions with us.

Some have probably seen the self-analysis type tests given by newspapers and magazines. The idea is to test attitudes on marriage, job, finances, etc. An RV magazine, in an article on full-timing, published such a test for potential full-timers. The test was structured in favor of adventure loving, gregarious, outgoing people. If you weren't looking forward to exploring the Alaskan Highway; if you enjoyed reading a novel more than an atlas; or if you called an expert for repairs; you were not a good candidate for full-timing. Likewise, if you would rather go to a flea market than visit a historic house, you would not score well on the test. We took the test and failed. Our score fell into the category that said, "Don't sell the house." This is pure rubbish. Full-timers represent a cross section of people. Thank goodness they are not all cut from the same mold. We have found full-timers who love to play bridge while others like poker or may hate cards all together. Some may go in for strenuous activities while others prefer to sit and visit. And there are those who watch soap operas on TV while others attend concerts or operas. Some may want to plan their travels solely around sightseeing, and there is nothing wrong with that. Others, however, will feel that full-timing is a lifestyle rather than a continual sightseeing lark, and that part of the fun is in the campground and the people who are there.

A week or two in any one campground seems to fly by. It takes that long to explore the immediate area, especially if there are several golf courses nearby. Since our budget does provide for dining out occasionally, we love to investigate the unusual and highly recommended restaurants. If they are inexpensive that is even better. Many campgrounds we stay at have recreational facilities and club house activities. We find that our days are kept busy with exploring the area, hiking, biking, walking, tennis, swimming, card playing, and just plain visiting. We try to walk four miles every day (usually before breakfast), and like to drive the back roads to see what there is to see—perhaps stopping in some little cafe for lunch.

These stops serve two purposes, namely lunch and a chance to meet the local people.

What time is left, has to be spent on housekeeping, laundry, meal preparation and routine maintenance. Although our "house" is small, there are things that have to be done. Curtains and windows have to be washed, clothes need laundering and vacuuming and dusting are regular chores. The vehicles also need to be washed and polished; the oil has to be changed, and the roof needs to be resealed once a year. Windows and vents have to be caulked occasionally, steps repainted, grill and lawn chairs cleaned, and on and on. Washing and polishing an RV can take a whole day.

A major activity in our household is the publishing of our bi-monthly newsletter. Originally, this was a two-page newsletter intended for family and a few close friends. It has now expanded to ten pages and many additional "subscribers." It's fun to do, but it is time consuming. We try to have it out on the first day of the month so the last few days of the month become panic time. The newsletter can definitely be considered a hobby, as it becomes fancier with each issue. It improves as our computer skill in word processing improves and with our ability to spend money on graphics software. It's easy to see that we are not bored.

Do full-timers have bad days? You bet they do! Many will remember the time at home when the washer and dryer went out at the same time, just after an expensive car repair? Those days happen to full-timers too. An RV has major appliances, and they are often more expensive to repair because they are compact and unique to the RV industry. Considering that full-timers are usually in strange territory, major mechanical repairs can be a concern when there is no experience with the repair facility. It is often necessary to rely on campground management or park neighbors for recommendations. The good news is that most appliances and replacement parts in the RV industry are standard. In the rare case that a part is not available, overnight express from the manufacturer can solve the problem. Most manufacturers are very cooperative when it comes to getting a part to full-timers because they understand that the RV is home. When our hot water heater needed replacement, it was accomplished in less than two hours. The frustration comes when we have something repaired and the work is guaranteed, but we are 1,000 miles away when it quits working. This is simply one of the disadvantages of our lifestyle. The handy person has the advantage here, because he/she can get the parts and take care of it themselves.

We will always remember the time we picked up a tank of bad gasoline in Los Angeles. In spite of three expensive service stops between California and New Mexico, our vehicle exhibited the same problem two or three hundred miles after each repair. After a tuneup in Las Vegas, Nevada (no help), and a carburetor rebuild job in Gallup, New Mexico (still no help), filter replacements and a fuel distribution valve replacement in Albuquerque, New Mexico, finally did the job —for 2,000 miles. Ultimately, the gasoline tank had to be taken off and cleaned. Usually, you have little or no recourse with the repair facility when you are several hundred miles down the road. In our case, an honest Ford dealer in Gallup, New Mexico, did refund the cost of the carburetor rebuilding. Those with mechanical ability may have avoided our frustration. We know handy folks who would have replaced filters right away and might even have had some with them. You see, one of us flunked that part of the full-timers aptitude test about fixing things. In our full-timing partnership the male partner's response is, "I'm more into the management and administrative end." This supports our position that there are, and should be, all types of full-timers. If one elects to sit in a lawn chair reading a book instead of washing the tow car or checking the oil, not to worry. Why should things be any different now?

Bad days don't have to evolve around mechanical problems either. Any number of things can go wrong when being a full-timer. Try two or three rainy cold weeks in a small RV parked in a remote location; and we can all relate to noisy neighbors. This can happen in a state forest campground or county park that's not patrolled. Better yet, three Volkswagen bus loads of flower children may decide to park in the next campsite. Commercial campgrounds can be disappointing too. However, in our full-timing experience, we have never had an unpleasant neighbor. If the day comes, and it probably will, we will simply move. Try *that* at home. We have found that the rangers and campground hosts at public parks continually monitor the campsites and will not hesitate to ask an unthinking camper to turn down a radio. Commercial and private membership parks are very careful to maintain a pleasant camping experience because their existence depends on it. Generally, campers are friendly and courteous people to be around. Most are also nature lovers and ecologically concerned. Our two months as volunteers at Hot Springs National Park in Arkansas taught us that. Campers left their sites spotless and were careful to maintain the beauty of the park. Daytime picnickers were not quite so careful.

One of our worst experiences started when we tarried too long at a mountain ranch and got caught in an overnight freeze that held at 17 degrees for over five hours. Since our drainage tanks were both open, they did not incur damage, but it took a long time to thaw the connecting hose and accomplish the outside work. The hose froze even though we left the water running slightly above a drizzle. Starting the night before, Barb was really feeling ill, a chronic bronchitis condition was worsened by the flu bug. Being concerned about her and the freeze up, Ron neglected to double check to see if the steering on our tow car was unlocked. It wasn't. About 20 miles down the road, concerned that the motorhome was pulling to the left, we realized that the problem might be with the tow car. Since the wheels were locked at a slight angle, the left front tire was already through rubber and showing wire cord. We continued, although not confident that we would reach a tire outlet before it let go. Meanwhile, Barb, laying down on the bed, was feeling much worse. Van Horn, Texas, was now about 40 miles away, and we hoped that they had a hospital or clinic. Van Horn is a small oasis type town between El Paso and Midland with not much more than the basic necessities. The day ended on a better note when we were directed to an excellent doctor who happened to be right across from a very fine RV park, which was next door to a pharmacy. The next morning the sun was out, and with the weather warming to the 60 degree range, we decided to sit for a couple of days and get Barb well. It was comforting to have the doctor right across the street. The RV park, by the way, charged $9 a night (1991 rate) including the Good Sam discount for a full hookup. We can't remember too many other bad days in our full-timing experience.

Not entirely bad, but definitely a nuisance are the little things. Whenever we pick a new town we need to find our way around. This is fine in the smaller towns, but not as easy in cities like Los Angeles, Salt Lake City, or Houston. We try to avoid the big cities, but it's not always possible. We have become great navigators.

Finding a grocery store can be a small problem and once the store is found, finding the isle with the salad dressing becomes the next challenge.

We try to make a game out of exploring, and have learned that it is helpful to find the visitor information center as we approach each new area. We are not afraid to ask questions and find that people are very helpful.

Telephones and the U.S. postal service have given us some headaches, but that happens in a home without wheels too. We figure this life can't be all fun; there has to be some frustration.

The good times are nearly every day. Honest!! This may sound romantic, but it is really true—each sunset, sunrise, new flower, new trail, new friend, new little town, friendly face in church all go to making our life more meaningful than ever

Barb On Guadalupe Peak

imagined. This country of ours is full of scenic wonders. We think of the Hill Country of Texas at wild flower time. We didn't know there were so many varieties of wild flowers—all the colors of the rainbow in every size and shape. We may never have experienced this if we weren't full-timers. We think back to Mount Rainier in Washington and how exciting it was to see the active glaciers at work, or the ink blue color of Crater Lake in Oregon with snow still on the ground in late August. We remember fondly the exhilaration of finally reaching Guadalupe Peak in West Texas. It had been a tough, steep climb, but the view was breathtaking and a bit scary; what a thrill to have made it to the top. The hike down was worse, and when we reached home, we were hungry and dirty, but too exhausted to do much more than go to bed. Still, it is one of the highlights of our life. The boat ride we took at sunset in the Everglades will remain with us as long as we live. The colors, the birds, and the fresh air were quite an experience!!

We have sampled life in a Southern Louisiana swamp where we met an alligator hunter. Douve described the hunting process and showed us how to skin a Nutria (muskrat looking animal). In Utah, we learned about the Mormons and spent hours searching our family trees in the Family History Library. Further south in Utah, we sampled the best pies we have ever eaten. We had never heard of pinto bean pie or pickle pie so we had to experience that too.

Have you ever had an occasion to do some spring or fall camping? Full-timers do a lot of that and most agree that it's the best time of the year. Granted, the weather may be cool, but the parks are deserted except for a few other rigs (probably full-timers) and occasionally a hearty tenter. We don't have to worry about getting a site; it's quiet, the rest rooms are empty and the hiking trails are deserted. We reflect on our good fortune and think about the rest of the population back at work or school. Sometimes the camping rates are even cheaper. Out-of-season camping is even possible in the Sun Belt. Many Gulf states such as Alabama, Mississippi, Louisiana and Texas have an abundance of camping sites open during the winter months. They are even available in Northern Florida, around Tallahassee, Panama City and Pensacola. Vacationers often consider these areas too cool for prime vacation spots, but full-timers like them because of the reasons mentioned above. Temperatures, on occasion, may dip into the twenties, but we know how to deal with that. Besides, we know that in a couple of days we will be on the golf course.

In discussing good and bad times, we have noted that full-timers are the same people who left the comfortable home on Elm Street, Anywhere, USA. After reviewing this chapter, we both agree that the good times far outnumber the bad times.

♥ ♥

LETTER TO THE EDITOR MOTORHOME MAGAZINE

[This letter appeared in Motorhome Magazine in the spring of 1991.

My husband and I have been happy full-timers for nearly two years. Not once in this time have we thought that we had made a mistake. Out of curiosity, though, I took Gaylord Maxwell's aptitude test (to determine our suitability to full-timing) on page 43 of the February issue of Motorhome Magazine. Four of my answers differed from HIS and for that, my score indicated that we should "Keep the house for a while." NO WAY!!!!

I double checked the questions we differed on and really got angry; not for me—but for all those who may think twice about full-timing just because of a low score on this one-sided aptitude test. Mr. Gaylord Maxwell is not a full-timer and obviously does not know that full-timers are not of one mold. Some like back roads, others like expressways. Some full-timers are handy; others call a repairman. Some like rustic out of the way places and do not like to be around people, while others have to be where there is lots of activity and many people to talk to. Some want to go to Alaska, some would take a trip to Europe, others just "Coast to Coast" along a few miles at a time. While full-timing, we parked our house (motorhome) for six weeks, took four panniers and our bicycles, flew to England and biked across England, Wales and Ireland, came home, jumped in the motorhome and resumed our full-timing. Can't full-timers want to go on a vacation just like other homeowners and retired people? Gaylord's question number 13 asked if we would like to see more of Europe, Asia, or the United States.

Who says one has to be a handyman to be a successful full-timer? Question seven indicates just that. We just had a hot water heater go and called a repairman. In my opinion, it is better to have professional repairs than have a botched up job if one is not mechanically inclined. Question number 22 also gives the reader the opinion that one who would rather carry favorite cassettes instead of a tool box is not a full-time type person. Sure, we carry a few minor tools, but they are not as important as our music on cassettes.

Gaylord's test suggests that full-timers must do away with material things. Yes, they give up their house and furniture, etc; but because people are all individuals, we have met full-timers who travel in luxury "homes" pulling luxury "pull toys," while camping only in the luxury campgrounds. At the other end of the spectrum, we live in a 24-foot class C, pull an old Horizon and like to camp in everything from the rustic to very nice campgrounds.

We see full-timers who only watch TV, seldom leave the campground and almost always travel the interstates. We also know the adventuresome full-timers who think nothing of taking off for parts unknown, camp alone in some national forest and take off on roads that aren't even on regular maps. Many others fall between these two extremes. Like the rest of the population, full-timers are all different. The only common thread that we can think of is that they must like their spouse. But that leaves out the single full-timers.

I hope that many who scored low on the test will think again and go for it. The only way you will know is to go out and do it. Bob Ramsey had the right idea. His letter (Missing Out) appeared on page eight of the same issue.

Sincerely,
Barbara Hofmeister

From the June 1991 issue of Movin' On

SO NEAR YET SO FAR

YOSEMITE NATIONAL PARK

On May 14, signs went up in the ranger station—"WINTER STORM WARNING—MAY 17 AND MAY 18."

Friday May 17 (my birthday) we had a day off. Because of the change in the campground, we took off to explore some of the out-of-park scenery. We had a most enjoyable day driving some remote roads in the nearby national forest. And for the first time since we arrived in the area, we could take advantage of the Friday night dinner at the Elks Club in Oakhurst.

The pouring rain we endured as we left Oakhurst, was heavy snow by the time we were back at camp. So they were right—it was winter again. Our awning was sagging with the heavy wet snow. We had just taken care of that and settled down to wait out the storm when a ranger knocked on our door. He brought us a message to call the Oak Flat entrance station; our son was there waiting for our call. I knew it must have been Robert coming from San Francisco to surprise me for my birthday. I was touched, but worried at the same time; the roads were so dangerous. I called immediately, and the rangers searched for him. While I waited, I could hear how busy they were. I overheard them telling people they could only get into the park with chains on, and that they had to wait and follow the snow plow. It sounded like mass confusion there, and when Karen got back on the phone, she reported that they couldn't find him.

I knew he couldn't get into the park because he didn't have chains and hoped he had gone far away from the snow. We waited up until midnight, just in case he got through. It is about 45 miles from Big Oak Flat to the Valley and on to Wawona (most of it at 6,000 feet). When it snows, it gets bad on that road.

In the morning it was no better. You'd expect snow, rain, and cold in winter, but not on May 18. Sunday, the storm broke and I was able to reach Robert on his ship at the Coast Guard Station. He was OK and had turned around just before we got the message. Since we had Monday and Tuesday off, we decided to take off and go to San Francisco to visit him. In no time, we had a suitcase packed and were

off. It felt so good to be away from the campground, and I wanted to see Robert. He had been so near—yet so far away. We were 80 miles from our destination and were getting onto the expressway to join the heavy traffic when Ron shifted down and lost 1st and 2nd gear. There was an exit right away, so we got off and headed back to the park. There was no way we could maneuver the hills of San Francisco with only third and fourth gear (also no reverse). We had no way of knowing what was going to drop next, and it was Sunday; no place would be open. It was very disappointing, and we rode in silence for miles. I cried; we were so close again. But, we came up with the idea of taking a vacation after we were finished in the campground before we started in the Pioneer Center. The car got fixed by our trusty friends at Gordon's; it was just the linkage, but took a week to get the parts.

So here we are in Coarsegold; I'll get the newsletter out and in the mail by Tuesday the 4th; then we will take our house and go to San Francisco. We are going to make it, Robert!

From the April 1990 issue of Movin' On.

BIG BEND
Beautifully Desolate

We had never really seen desert before arriving at Big Bend on March 31. Dry, magnificent and barren are just a few of the words that could describe this remote, 801,000-acre park. First of all, it seems like a million miles from nowhere. The park, located in the southwest part of Texas, is right on the Rio Grande River and 103 miles from the nearest full service town. The little village of Marathon to the north of the park was over 80 miles from our campground and it didn't have a grocery store. We were well prepared for our ten-day visit with lots of groceries. There was a little store at each of the three campgrounds in the park, but just basics were sold at rather high prices.

Big Bend offers much to do. Each evening, at the Rio Grande Village Campground Amphitheater, a ranger presented a terrific slide show and talk on the park. They were on a variety of interesting subjects such as, the history of man in Big Bend, geology of the park, how the plants and animals of the desert adapt to the lack of water and predators, bats and birds. The programs were well attended, probably, because there was nothing else to do there. We were too far away for TV reception and couldn't get an English speaking radio station.

Big Bend is a park of contrasts—the desert, the mountains and the lush areas next to the Rio Grande River. There was a lot to see. Driving and hiking was the only way to see anything. Either way meant a lot of driving. We drove the 50 plus miles to go to the canyon at the southwest end of the park. Once we arrived at the canyon, the only way to see it was to hike in over the canyon wall and down into the gorge. Although the hike and drive were long, it was well worth it. That was typical of all the hikes. We tried to get to the *Grapevine* trail head, but gave up after driving 6.2 miles down the unimproved road. The park is full of these roads, and many who visit the park have "high clearance" vehicles, such as trucks and Blazers. We did make it down the road to the hot springs and enjoyed soaking in the hot bubbly waters right on the banks of the river. It always seemed strange to look across the narrow river and see Mexico minus any evidence of it being another country.

We did go to the border town of

Boquillas by way of a row boat. We sat in the boat while the young Mexican boy walked in the water pulling us across. That little village has no electricity, and the adobe houses are without windows and doors. I never saw such poverty, but everyone seemed happy, including the children.

Hiking in Big Bend was a new adventure for us. The desert hiking wasn't difficult, except for the heat, and the sights of cactus in bloom made the walks fascinating. Up in the mountains of the park our hikes took on a new dimension. We hiked several long, strenuous trails. One, to "The Window" was only five miles, but the trip back was all up hill. After resting a day or two, we thought we could handle the six and one half mile "Lost Mine" trail. The hike was so beautiful that I will remember it for a long time. We started from our campground (elevation 1,200 feet) and drove the 23 miles to the trail head at Basin Junction. That drive alone was spectacular, because in those short miles you drive from the barren desert to pine covered mountains. Then we hiked up another 1,000 feet along beautiful Douglas Fir covered slopes enjoying the cool clear air. We were basically alone on the trail and felt at peace with nature. The rangers had warned us to be on the look out for some young aggressive panthers, but we only saw and heard the most beautiful birds; and when we reached the top and looked down, the view was breathtaking. Before we started back down, we rested and ate our packed lunch. Wonderful!!! I can't wait to see the pictures and relive the day.

Back down the hill at the campground we couldn't believe the temperature difference. Usually there is at least a 20 degree difference between the mountains and the desert. By the way, the average summer temperature is 120 degrees. Few visit the park in the summer, but the rangers and their families have to stay. The dependent children of the rangers, attend a park service country school up to the eighth grade. After that, the ranger has to get transferred. And don't forget the 103-mile trip for groceries or the doctor, dentist, etc. Our visit to the park was another terrific learning experience.

From the December 1991 Issue of Movin' On

BIG WINNER

Ron and Barb had spent a week in Las Vegas and had fun doing all the things one does in that city. As they were leaving, Barb remarked that she had had enough gambling and staying out late. Ron agreed. They got all settled at the Coast to Coast campground in Needles, California, and although it advertised being close to Laughlin, Nevada, these two agreed that they weren't interested. They had been to Laughlin earlier in the year.

One of the places they wanted to visit was Oatman, Arizona, so Sunday after church they took off. They spent the afternoon enjoying this lively ghost town. They left for home and at the T intersection saw that they had a choice of going back to Needles or just a few miles to Laughlin. "Why not?," Ron said. "Lets go and have the $3.89 buffet at the casino," and off they went.

Along the way, billboards advertised, **"Every Room only $19.00"** (at the Edgewater—one of the Circus Circus casinos). "Why not?," Barb said, "It'll be kind of fun and we would gamble $19 away anyway." So, full of anticipation and excitement at being so impulsive, they drove the short distance to this friendly casino town.

They joked when, checking in without luggage, that they would have the bell captain get it later. Truth was they didn't even have a comb or tooth brush, let alone luggage. After getting settled (?) in the room, they went to dinner.

Now that they were going to be in the casino for the evening, they thought they would try their luck for awhile. Barb watched the Roulette tables but didn't like the numbers coming up. Both tried a little black jack and weren't successful. "If I lose five hands in a row, I leave the table," Barb said. So it was, that they sat side by side at the quarter poker machines. Shortly after they sat down to play, the bells and lights went off just behind them. A lady got a royal flush, which is the big payoff on the poker machines. Ron and Barb kept getting full houses and even four of a kind. When either got to draw to three high cards in the same suit, they told each other so they'd have help cheering for a Royal Flush. But the right cards never come up.

Ron put the last five quarters, he was going to play, into the machine (they play five at a time) and got a King, Queen, and Jack of Spades. He didn't bother telling Barb and drew two cards. Up came the Ace and Ten of Spades. Ron said, "I thought I had a flush, but the bells and lights told me it was a Royal Flush." Ron started hollering, "I hit it, I hit it, I did it, it's a Royal Flush." It only took a few seconds for Ron to figure that 4,000 quarters equals $1,000. Soon the attendant came over and gave Ron 10 crisp new $100 bills. Later Ron said that he had considered the small losses as entertainment, so it was no big deal, but now this put him way ahead and that was a good feeling. "Getting lucky doesn't always happen to the other guy."

Ron's luck continued the next morning when the two played the poker machines again. He won an additional $50. All in all, it was an exciting evening. Barb said, "Our life is exciting anyway, but this was really something special. To me, it was just fun to check into the motel without any luggage. I felt like a kid. Everyone needs to do something like this once in a while and the fact that we got rewarded for it, proves it was the right thing to do."

♥ ⌂ ♥

13

MAKING CHANGES

Life is full of changes, and full-timers experience their share. We are no different from others, who for some reason or other, make changes in their lives. For retirees, whether full-timers or not, some decisions remain the same. It may be time to sell the old homestead. Many retirees consider taxes, heating bills, and maintenance, too much to handle on a large home that they no longer need. They find it easier to buy or rent a smaller home or condo in their hometown. Since the decision to full-time is not irreversible, the switch to a smaller living unit can always be made when full-timing days are over. If the decision is to full-time, the funds tied up in a building could be earning interest. The days of rapid appreciation of a home appear over, at least for the immediate future. Granted, the interest rates aren't that great either, but at least all options remain open.

We have been making changes since we started full-timing.

197

In spite of the planning that was discussed in Chapter 7, we found that we needed to make some changes in our clothing selections and household items. We were over-packed on dress clothes, and in spite of being in the South, found that we needed more of our warmer clothes. All Sunbelt states have plenty of cool/cold days in the winter months. The sun sets early and tee-shirts and shorts don't work well in the evenings. We quickly learned that we needed all of our long sleeve shirts, sweat shirts and pullovers.

On our first motorhome, we learned about solar panels and added one of them to our roof. Later, we bought a small generator to supplement the solar panel. These two items, plus awnings and roof storage pods, are common additions.

We changed our style of traveling after just a few months. At first, we were in such a hurry to see everything that we moved often. We had given our family and friends an itinerary and felt we had to live up to it; but, the pressure we put on ourselves was too much. After a few months, we tore up the itinerary and started to move less often.

At first, visiting state and national parks was our primary goal. When we discovered Camp Coast to Coast and their affordable luxuries, we changed directions. Now we camp primarily in those campgrounds. We haven't given up on the public parks—we mix it up. We added volunteering, and these changes made a positive difference in our lifestyle.

We have met full-timers who buy a new rig every year. Dealers make it easy to move into a new RV home. The new buyer parks his old rig on their lot, next to the new house. Then, all he has to do is move next door. We have heard from many who have moved this way and all had pleasant experiences. The dealers let them stay for as long as it takes to ensure there are no problems with the new rig.

It is not uncommon for full-timers to purchase new towing vehicles, but if keeping the old vehicle, it may be necessary to make some mechanical adjustments. For example, when pulling a large unit, it may be helpful to install a transmission cooling unit. If a tow car is not tracking well, or the connections are proving too cumbersome, changes will have to be made. Some decide to change from towing on all four wheels to using a tow dolly or vice versa. Eventually, we found it very convenient to tow a small pickup with a cap on the truck bed for additional storage.

Making changes in familiar territory is often helpful because mechanics, dealers and suppliers are better known. On the other hand, we didn't have a bit of trouble when we bought our new tow vehicle in Oregon (2,000 miles away from familiar dealers). We have had warranty work done in California, and again in Texas, with no problems at all.

We changed our mail forwarding address while on the road and it was no different from any other time in our life when we had to make that change. It did seem strange to go through all that trouble when we didn't really move. We sent out notices to everyone on our correspondence list and made the transition within two months.

In December 1992, we made a major change—the purchase of a new 34-foot Bounder motorhome. We were both ready for the luxury of more room and all the furnishings and equipment that went with it. Since we still move a lot, a motorhome seemed to be the best choice for our needs, but we reserve the right to change our minds sometime in the future. There will be a time when our moving will be less frequent with fewer miles traveled. We think that with this approach, full-timing can continue well into the golden years. To carry this to the extreme, imagine a roomy fifth-wheel that is moved only twice a year. During the summer months, it could be parked at a serene, northern lake and then moved to a warm Sunbelt location for the winter.

Several full-timing friends of ours are beginning the construction of an RV pad on acreage that they own not far from their original home. The location will include a storage building next to the pad and all the hookups. They are also considering an RV-tall carport type roof for weather protection. Shrubs and trees will be planted around the site so, for them, this could be the best of both worlds. They will be near family, friends and old surroundings, while remaining independently mobile and comfortable in their RV home. They will not have to worry about campground arrangements or parking in relatives' driveways. When the snow starts to fly, their comfortable home will move South, where other friends await them. They are still full-timers.

It's time for us to have a storage locker sale. It took us four years to realize that we really don't need to rent that large storage unit. We no longer need the security blanket of the many items we saved. Everyone will think differently in this respect. Some may want to make a storage adjustment after the first trip. Some may not even have gone the storage route to begin with.

There may be other adjustments along the way. These adjustments will occur more frequently in the first few months. It's a fun learning experience if viewed as an adventure. We have found that a good source of information is other full-timers. They are easy to find because of their rigs. If their RV has campground membership decals, Escapee and Good Sam decals, a Family Motor Coach membership plate, large storage pods, solar panels, and a small ladder attached on the rear, chances are good that they are full-timers. We have yet to find full-timers or other RVers who are not anxious to share experiences. They love to talk about their RV, special equipment, favorite campground or restaurant, and local points of interest. The list goes on. What is the best RV battery, generator, solar panel, or towing truck (diesel or gasoline)? Where is the closest laundromat, the best supermarket or shopping center? Most will proudly offer to show the inside of their rig and share their experience with that particular model or others that they have owned.

Another good source of information may come from someone who owns an identical RV. It will be interesting to see how they have utilized available space, or added little shelves and other conveniences. On one such inspection we learned that owners of a rig identical to our first motorhome, increased their bathroom space with a simple adjustment. We also copied them on the utilization of wall space. The same couple showed us a neat way to put a closure spring on our screen door. This involved stretching an inexpensive screen door spring on the door over the outside hinge, and attaching it with a metal screw on each end. The best part of learning from others is the friendship that we make while doing so.

At the beginning of this book, we said that the decision to full-time was not irreversible. There may come a time when it is physically unwise to continue as a full or part-timer. Who, more than the full-timer, knows the best place in the United States to settle down. With friends all over the country and an excellent knowledge of retiree havens, full-timers are in a good position to make a nesting choice that meets their needs. That choice may even be their original home base where family are located. RVs are just as easy to sell as houses (probably easier), and the transition to a small apartment or condo should not be difficult for those used to living in an RV. Our problem will be to pick one spot from all of the beautiful places we have visited. Western Montana, Northern Arizona, Central Texas, and Southwestern Arkansas all beckon to us as permanent retirement sites. In the next ten years we will add many more to the list. It's a tough life.

♥   ♥

From the September 1991 issue of Movin' On

NEW PULL TOYOTA
For the Hofmeisters

Can you believe it? Ron and Barb got rid of the poor ole Horizon. On August 14 they took possession of a new 1991 white Toyota pickup truck, complete with pretty white shell (cap or canopy —whatever you want to call it). It was all wired up for towing and the Yakima bike racks were firmly in place.

Just a few days after the last newsletter went out, so did the car. This time it was a wiring problem; a short in the fan caused wires to burn. The result was that the car died. Ron and Barb decided that they would let the car sit for the two weeks they had left and then simply tow it out of Yosemite. Ron made an appointment at a Chrysler dealer in Lodi, California, which was a fair sized town near their first destination (Isleton, CA).

The car was delivered by 8:00 a.m. Monday, July 29, but not repaired until Wednesday the 31st (parts had to be ordered). The cost including three hours of work to find the short amounted to $250. Once repaired, Ron remarked that the ole car seemed to be in really good condition now—nothing else could possibly go wrong. Barb shook her head; she had heard that one before.

They drove that brown bomb all over Napa Valley and into San Francisco, towed it up to the Redwoods and drove all around that area—even on some pretty raw dirt roads. It seemed OK.

Sunday, August 11, the Hofmeisters crossed the border into Oregon and set up camp in a Coast to Coast campground in Talent. Since it was early in the day, they took off to explore the surrounding area. Ashland seemed to be the most interesting and the closest, so they headed there, parked and walked around. But as they were leaving, Ron put the car into reverse and let out the clutch to hear some awful noises and a lot of jerking. It was happening again—clutch or transmission or both. They looked at each other and immediately decided to drive to Medford and *look* in the car lots.

Ron had originally thought of waiting until they got to Eugene (larger city) and until that moment was even thinking they could get by without buying a new vehicle.

It was easy to see that Medford was a good sized town with lots of auto dealers. The big three and all the Japanese brands were available. They were browsing in the Toyota lot when, to their surprise, a sales-person appeared. Unlike Michigan, dealerships are open Saturday and Sunday. After talking a little and getting a base price, they left promising to return on Monday. They drove around the corner to the Nissan dealer and talked to the salesmen there. Both had nice trucks and the price was about what Ron had figured.

Early Monday morning Barb and Ron were at the Toyota dealer. The negotiating began and went on till noon. Since the truck was stripped down and they wanted air, radio, carpeting and seat covers, deals had to be made. Then the dealer drove the Horizon before giving a trade-in price. All they were willing to give for it (they were going to wholesale it) was $200. Ron said, "NO, all the new parts are worth more." In true salesmen fashion, he asked what Ron needed. "$500," Ron said. There was a conference somewhere and when the salesman returned he said $400 was his very best, but he juggled something else somewhere and the bottom line was now acceptable to Ron.

Salesman Rich took the pair to Kountry Kampers to pick out the canopy, but later when they went to pick it up, the off-white top clashed badly with the stark white of the truck. Barb had seen Truck Tops Plus and went there. Julie was super and they got a much better top and information on installing the bike rack on the canopy. Julie fixed them up at a modest cost of $45 (for rain gutters), guaranteed the work for the life of the truck, and the bike rack fit nicely.

By calling the RV dealers advertised in Trailer Life Campground Directory, they found that Mike, at Triple A RV could wire the new truck for towing and squeeze them into their busy schedule. The job they did was very professional —100% better than the job that had been done on the Horizon. Total cost was $214.

Barb said it was fun getting the back-end all organized, and they enjoyed the air conditioning since the temperature was nearly 100 degrees every day. They said it was even fun to be able to listen to a radio—the one in the Horizon broke long ago. But both agree that the best part is knowing that they have dependable transportation.

Ron was a little nostalgic about that old Horizon. He hadn't had a new car in a long time when he bought it in 1983. Barb remembers that she had to furnish the transportation on their first date (October 5, 1983); he took delivery of his car the next day. At any rate this closes the book on the ole Horizon.

♥ ⌂ ♥

14

FINAL THOUGHTS

We have discussed, at length, the social and economic impacts of full-timing, as well as changes that will ultimately occur. Since Ron writes a potpourri column in our monthly newsletter, we thought it would be helpful if he ended the book with a few of his thoughts that may eventually find their way into his monthly column. Besides, we didn't want to end the book with a Chapter 13, thus this extra chapter at no cost. Early on in this book, we made a disclaimer relative to the mechanical aspect of maintaining an RV while living on the road. It's true that Ron is not mechanically inclined, and his best friends will readily attest to that. That is why the following suggestions should not carry any more weight than information gained across the fence or, in our case, across the campsite.

For what they're worth. . .

■ To avoid fuel contamination, buy fuel from a large busy station—doesn't always work, but the odds are better.

■ Shopping center and church parking lots are great places to stop for lunch or coffee breaks while traveling.

■ Cheap toilet paper is just as good as the very expensive special RV toilet paper sold at RV supply stores.

■ 12 volt RV light bulbs can be purchased in the automotive section of a discount chain store at a great saving.

■ Rotate the cushions in the dinette area in order to retain firmness. Even the best grade of foam will eventually break down and need to be replaced. Go to any upholstry place and buy an extra, extra firm grade after two years or so. Each cushion will cost under $40 to redo.

■ Make the RV look like home. Plants, little lamps and pictures will do it. We even put our grandchildren's drawings on the refrigerator.

■ Two inch thick boards about two feet long and a foot wide work well for leveling motorhomes. That is, unless you can afford automatic leveling jacks. Boards cost $10 at a building supply center. They will even cut them for you.

■ Sewer hoses are cheap ($10). Don't try to patch them.

■ Carry an extra water hose, preferably 50 feet. They are great for washing vehicles without unhooking the RV water supply. In some campground sites the extra hose may be needed for water hookup. We carry a 25 foot hose, which works for most hookups, plus a 50 foot hose to use when necessary.

- Likewise, carry an extra electrical cord. We carry several along with conversion plugs to accommodate the different campground hookups. Most have both the two and three prong receptacles, but a few do not, particularly some of the public parks.

- A small brass water regulator costing $10, available at any RV store, is essential. It screws on between the faucet and your hose and will prevent high pressure water (common) from damaging your RV water tubing.

- You may also want to carry a small water filter attachment with replaceable filters. This also attaches to your outside source and can be obtained at most hardware or RV supply stores for about $20. We have one, and have used it occasionally in rusty water areas.

- Carrying a small electric heater (1500 watt) will add to your comfort and save you money. It allows you to save your propane and use campground electricity instead. It also supplements your propane furnace when it's extremely cold, not to mention a backup if the furnace fails. There are many articles in the RV magazines on alternative heating appliances, including the popular ceramic heaters. Investigate and ask your RV neighbor.

- Keep a quarter dish in your RV where you can collect quarters every night from your change. You will use a lot of them for newspapers, laundromats and telephones. A 35mm film canister holds about six dollars worth.

- Magazine racks that can be attached to a wall or cupboard are a great investment in reducing clutter. They can be purchased at an RV supply store.

■ Not all RV dealers are knowledgeable about solar panels. They are great if installed properly. It took us a year to realize that ours wasn't installed correctly—what a difference when it was. Find out how many your dealer has installed.

■ A handy box or bag of rags is helpful. Outside hoses, cords and boards need to be wiped when put away.

■ A lighter stick fueled with lighter fluid or butane is helpful in lighting water heaters and other appliances that don't have automatic ignition. They can be purchased at most RV stores.

■ A small rubber pad used for opening jar tops works well for tightening and loosening water hose connections.

■ A voltage meter is essential. We keep ours plugged into the wall socket in the bathroom. They cost between $15 and $20. Many campgrounds have low voltage that can damage appliances. If voltage is below 110, it is best to keep your refrigerator on propane and not use other appliances.

■ A caulking gun with silicone caulking is a handy tool to carry. Annual caulking around RV windows, doors and compartments will prevent leaks. This can be done leisurely on a nice sunny day.

■ Roof seams and areas around equipment installations, need to be resealed once a year. It is a ten-minute job, and roof sealant is available at any RV supply store. Buy only a quart, because you will not use more than that, and a gallon (although cheaper) is a pain to store.

■ Unless you really want one, avoid the large green outdoor rugs that attract dirt and moisture. A small mat will do nicely. Keep it simple.

■ Likewise, avoid accumulating things. Knickknacks, cutesy yard signs and windmills all take time to put away when traveling and take up precious storage space.

■ Since we love to cook outdoors, a small compact barbecue is handy to carry. Ours uses very little charcoal, because when done, we close it up tight and the unused charcoal stops burning (no oxygen).

■ We also carry a camp stove that operates on a small propane cylinder. It's compact and slides into an outside storage compartment. When it's hot we tend to cook outside under the awning.

■ Portable lanterns are handy to have, especially if you are dry camping or in a public park. We like ours, even if we have electricity, because it gives us a soft camping light on those nights when we spend a lot of time outdoors.

■ Did you know that many commercial and membership campgrounds have a book exchange library? You just drop off a paperback that you have read and pick up another one. However, please don't drop this book off, because it will cut into our sales.

■ When traveling it is safer to shut off propane appliances and the outside propane valve. This is especially true when filling the vehicle with fuel. Even if you travel for eight hours (not recommended), the refrigerator and freezer will stay cold.

■ Buy good lawn chairs and ones that fold flat for easy storage. They will last longer, unless they get too many sparks from the campfire (like ours).

■ Spouses need to work as a team when backing the RV.

Work out a set of signals and practice them. Better yet, practice patience and understanding. Many marriages have been strained over the backing and positioning of an RV.

■ Never leave the RV for long periods with the awning down, especially in the west. Strong winds come up suddenly and an expensive awning can be destroyed in minutes.

■ When in a full hookup, do not leave the black water valve open to the sewer outlet. It is best to keep it closed with at lease three or four gallons of water in the tank in order to keep solids from collecting on the bottom. It can then be emptied every few days.

■ It's best to use a full grey water tank for flushing after emptying the black water. Closing the valve just before taking showers gives a good supply of warm water.

■ After dumping and just before traveling, dump some water and add a large bag of ice cubes through the toilet into the black water holding tank. The cubes will help loosen some dried on materials while traveling and melt with no ill effects.

■ Free maps are available at all state welcome centers. Also available in most states, are nice color books which detail every part of the state. These books are not out in the open so you have to ask for them. Texas has the very best one.

■ It's a good idea to find out in what county you are staying. Unless they are in an area for some time, most travelers don't know and weather alerts on radio and television are designated by county.

■ You can own your own weather alert system by investing in a hand held gadget called, "Weatheradio Alert." It is manufactured by Realistic and distributed by Radio Shack.

Continuous weather information is broadcast from the National Weather Service. When the alarm is set, it will go off when severe weather is forecast.

■ Regular household silicone is great for keeping objects from moving around the RV while traveling. Put a small amount of silicone on the bottom of the object and allow it to dry. Small photo frames and knickknacks will stand straight when traveling.

■ And last but not least, be a thoughtful camper by following a few basic unwritten rules.

✓ Never cut through another's campsite even if it means walking a little further. It's their yard.

✓ When traveling keep an eye out for long lines of traffic piling up behind you and pull over on the pulloffs as often as possible to let traffic pass.

✓ Dump grey and black water at designated dump stations only and rinse the dump area if necessary when finished.

✓ When dry camping in public parks where many campers are tenters, please limit the use of your generator. Listen to the sounds of nature rather than TV and instead of using electrical appliances (microwave, toaster etc), do things the old fashioned way for an enjoyable experience for everyone.

The above list is by no means complete. The rest you have to experience. We hope that you will experience the joys of full-timing and view it as an adventure.

♥ ♥

From the April 1990 issue of Movin' On.

BEANCOUNTER

TRIES

TO BECOME

HANDYMAN

MISSION, TEXAS Ron Hofmeister spent a good part of three weeks attempting to do much needed work on his motorhome and car. It is a well-known fact among his family and friends that Ron does not know the difference between a screwdriver and a hammer—much less what to do with them, but he seemed determined to become Mr. Fix-it. Several things needed attention. Both of the vehicles needed washing to remove the salt from the visit to Padre Island. The bikes needed a good cleaning and some rust removal. The roof of the motor home had leaked badly, near the front vent, during a recent rain storm (Ron was sure that it was a fluke or just the way the wind was blowing). The holding tank (sewer) had been leaking for months and was getting worse, and the entry step was more rust than paint. Ron also wanted to shop for a generator before he headed into the remote camping ahead (the solar panel needed help). "There's more work in a motorhome than there is in a house," he said as he faced the jobs.

Shortly after arriving in Mission, Ron tackled the vehicle washing. "I'm glad that we happened to pick a park with asphalt pads, double water connections and no restrictions on car washings—I can really get a lot of work done here," he told his wife, Barbara. The vehicles were washed right away with lots of supervision from all the guys nearby. Even the entry step was sanded and painted within a week. Shortly after that Ron took care of his bike. After each job was done, he needed to rest for two days. The holding tank repair kit had been purchased months ago. Ron was waiting for just the "right"(?) conditions.

The roof was a different story—

he said he needed to talk to lots of different people before deciding what to do about it. They went to a big RV parts and equipment place to purchase the generator, but Barb could not get Ron interested in even looking into the roof stuff nor would he talk to anyone there about it. That same night Barb noticed some strange bumps on the ceiling in the corner of the cab area. It was lots of fungus growing, and although Ron wanted her to ignore it for a few days, she immediately removed the wallpaper there so the wood could dry. It was saturated and it had been weeks since it had rained. The wet spot was a good two feet from the vent where the water had dripped in during the last rain storm. Barb said the roof needed attention—**NOW!**

The next day, Ron went back to the RV place and easily found the product he needed (roof sealer) and vowed to fix both the holding tank and the roof in the same day. First thing (**two days later with rain predicted**), Ron climbed up to the roof and in no time had that sealed. He even glued down the TV antenna in the process.

After he read the tank repair directions, he said, "It says it is a 20 minute job—that means 40 for me." Barbara went for a 40 minute walk. When she returned, he told her that he "botched the job." The repair material is fiberglass and once mixed, hardens in just five minutes. Ron had mixed it while sitting in the lawn chair on the other side of the motorhome, then walked to the tank, crawled under and had just started to apply the stuff when it hardened.

Barbara went to the store and bought another kit. She mixed it this time and finished the area that he had started. When it was set, and water was put in the tank—it still leaked just as bad as ever. He had "fixed" a spot that wasn't the leak. The crack was further up and quite large. Back to the store—one more kit—one more try. This time Barb did the work and Ron was the helper. They think they will make it until they get back to Jessie at Dennis Trailer Sales in Lansing. Barb said, "I knew that he wasn't a handy kind of guy when I married him and I still love him. I will admit that I am learning how to fix a lot of things in our motorhome."

Post script 1993. When we traded in the motorhome, the repair job was still holding fine.

From the February 1991 issue of Movin' On

HANDYMAN STRIKES AGAIN

Last year you may remember that while in Mission, Ron got into some big repair projects and one of them made a very funny story (the holding tank repair caper). Ron's handyman skills have greatly improved. Maybe someday he will even write a handyman's guide book.

The front vent had broken in one of the Valley's wind storms and, undaunted, Ron went to Camping World, bought a new vent, climbed right up on the roof and proceeded to unscrew everything. He replaced the vent, put it all back together and no parts were left over. He did a good job.

His best job was the water heater repair. After our neighbor informed us that we were gushing water all over the place, Ron and the neighbor discovered that we had a hole in our hot water heater. Ron and Ray successfully shut off the water supply to the heater and kibitzed about the problem. Ray told Ron that the heater could be easily replaced. Without blinking an eye, Ron went straight to the phone and called a repairman. You would have been proud of how well he wrote the check for $272. Didn't even get his hands dirty.

♥ ⌂ ♥

APPENDIX A

MORE FROM MOVIN' ON

We have fun reporting on all the exciting places we have been and especially all the new friends we meet. It breaks our heart that we do not have enough room to share all of the stories—especially the *Interesting People* stories. We wish that you could meet some of the people we have met, primarily those we wrote about. Since we are limited in space, we can only share one of those here, but we included several of our travel stories.

From the Sept 1990 issue

WHAT A CAMPER

We met Mr. Laverne F. Curtis at *Muskallonge State Park* in Michigan's Upper Peninsula. He was camping with our friends Gerald and Carolyn Branch and their children, Becky and Brian. The four Branches camped in their pop-up camper and Mr. Curtis along with his daughter, Joyce, camped nearby in a tent. Mr. Curtis is 94 years old and is Carolyn's grandfather. His daughter is Carolyn's 65 year old mother. Mr. Curtis loves to camp, explore, swim, dance, walk, hike, read and loves roller coasters (he last rode the Blue Streak at Cedar Point, Ohio, when he was 90). He acts and looks like a much younger man. When asked to what he attributed his longevity, he said that

he didn't know. His father died of cancer at 26.

Breakfast for most of his life has been an egg, oatmeal, toast and coffee. He walks at least two miles a day, but when he is at his home in Florida, he prefers to do his walking at night (10-11 pm) when it is cooler. Until just recently, he rode a bicycle daily. He seldom goes to bed before midnight and likes to get up early. He proved that while camping by staying with us until the campfire was only a glow each evening and being "up and at'em" bright and early each morning. And that was after spending cold (45⁰) and sometimes rainy nights in the tent.

He walked the stoney beaches of Lake Superior, searching for pretty stones, or good kindling for the campfire and was an asset to the men's Boccie ball team (they won all the games).

Mr. Curtis has lived alone in St. Petersburg, Florida since 1957 when he became a widower. His wife was an invalid for 17 years before her death and he took complete care of her. When he is at home, he eats lunch out everyday and usually at a buffet so he can have a wide variety of foods. In the evening he just fixes a snack. He comes up to Michigan in the summer to visit his only daughter, grandchildren and great grandchildren.

Most campers I know, like to fish. Not Mr. Curtis. "No time for fishing," he said. He is too busy. He left Muskallonge early Saturday morning to head back to Lansing (6-hour drive) because he wanted to go to his Saturday night dance in Holt. He goes every Saturday night, dances from 9:30 to midnight then drives back to his daughter's home. Dancing is his first love and he is fussy about his partners. If he asks a woman to dance and finds she is not a good dancer, she won't get asked by him again. When asked if he had ever thought about remarrying, he gave an emphatic, "No."

Just this last spring, Mr. Curtis had trouble breathing during a weekend. He waited until Monday morning, drove himself to the doctor's office, was immediately sent to the hospital and put into ICU. He had had a massive heart attack. You certainly wouldn't know it to look at him now. It was delightful to talk with him and hear stories of his childhood and the years before his wife had a stroke. He was born July 18, 1896 in Marshall, Michigan. For a little while after WW1, He worked for Reo Motors but didn't like that. He became a postal employee and kept that job until retirement.

One night while we were camping, Mr. Curtis left the campfire at 9:30 p.m.. Everyone thought he had gone for a walk. When he hadn't returned by 10:30, the family became worried and were ready to go searching for him. Just then, he nonchalantly walked to the campsite. Joyce greeted him with, "Daddy, where have you been?" He was quite surprised at her concern and explained rather indignantly that he had been in the rest room reading his book. Since he only had four more chapters to go, and it was dark out, he simply went where there was light. What a neat gentleman!

Post Script: Mr. Curtiss is still alive and well and living alone in Florida.

From The May 1990 Issue of Movin' On

WE CLIMBED GUADALUPE PEAK
And Lived to Tell About it

As we left *Big Bend National Park* in Texas, and drove north toward New Mexico, we saw more desert. Miles and miles of colorful blossoming cactus stuck into dry flat earth was all we saw until a mountain appeared in front of us. We saw it far in the distance and drove straight at it for more than twenty miles. It seemed as though we would never get close to it. The big red mountain whose peak reached far up into the clouds was *Guadalupe Peak*. As soon as we parked our house in the campground (which was just a parking lot), we checked with a ranger on the hikes available. We were only going to be able to do one hike, so we wanted to take the best one. The ranger suggested the scenic nine-mile canyon hike, but I kept looking at the information about the hike to the peak and thinking about that mountain. Driving to it, as we had done, I couldn't get it out of my mind. I wanted to touch it. I rationalized that it was only a few miles longer than the longest

hike we had done at Big Bend. I really felt up to the challenge and talked Ron into it. The peak stood at an elevation of 8,749 feet and we were at a little over 5,000 feet in the campground where the trail began. Our climb would be over 3,000 feet and we were told that our 8 ½ mile hike should take us six to eight hours round trip. We started out full of excitement early the next morning. Our canteens were full of water and we had our backpacks filled with lunch and other nourishing goodies. We also carried our cameras, binoculars and walking sticks and I was wearing my new *Reebok Ladies Rugged Walker* shoes that I broke in nicely at Big Bend.

The climb was dramatic, daring and spectacular. It was so steep at the beginning that the calves of my legs tightened right up. Now I knew why we had to sign a log book at the beginning of the trail; **this was a real climb.** Good thing that we had our walking sticks. The switchback trail snaked along and up and in no time, the campground below looked like a toy parking lot. We were going up quickly, but we were nowhere near the top of the first peak, and it wasn't the one that we set out to conquer. Guadalupe Peak was beyond and a lot higher. After one hour, we were on the back of the first peak and could see our destination—still so far up. Looking down from this point was scary. I couldn't believe that I had subjected myself to such a hike when I am afraid of anything higher than a roller coaster. The mountain trails that we had been on in Big Bend seemed like casual walks now and there were always lots of trees so that I couldn't see straight down hundreds of feet. On some parts of this trail, we were walking on a narrow ledge which encircled the mountain and looking down was a sheer drop. A looooooong way down.

We met a few other hikers—one was coming down already and two passed us when we were on the way up. They were a lot younger. By the way, on the whole climb up and down, we only counted 11 others who did it that day and 10 of them were young men. The one female was in her early 20's. We had started out at 8 a.m. and reached the summit a little before noon. The view was awesome. I kidded that we could see Houston from there. Ron said, "No, I think we can see Florida." The two guys who

passed us were still up there taking pictures. Both were good climbers and one (Adrian) plans to climb to the highest peak in each state. He practically ran up and down the hill (I don't know what his hurry was). Adrian is planning to do Mt Everest soon. We were in good company right? Besides the view at the top, there was a metal box and inside a ledger book where all who climbed could sign their name. We now have our name in the "summit box" on Guadalupe Peak—8749 feet up in the air.

The climb down was just as difficult as the climb up, mainly because it was so steep. It would be OK for a little while, but four miles of steepness stretches the leg muscles in ways that are not natural. The top of my toes blistered from rubbing against my shoes. We were down by 3:30 and we just collapsed at home for a while—too tired to even take our shoes off. Once we got the energy to shower, we felt a little better. Dinner was instant soup and we were in bed by 8:30. You are probably asking why we would torture our bodies so, and I cannot give you an answer. It was just there beckoning me to touch it. At least we can say that we did it. All the others came down looking just as beat as we felt. But we were the only ones even near our age to climb Guadalupe peak that day.

From the Sept 1990 issue

GRAND MARAIS, MICHIGAN
A Little Bit Of Heaven On Lake Superior

If you were driving through Grand Marais, Michigan, and saw the sailboats lounging in it's picturesque harbor, the main street with only a few old stores and, further along the coast an old Coast Guard Station, you might want to visit for a little while before going on your way. And if you did stop in at the general store or the market place, it would only take you a short time to see everything there. If you happened to be in Grand Marais between one and four p.m. on Tuesday through Saturday, you might venture out to the Coast Guard Station, which is now a museum, and enjoy a personal tour of the restored home. There is a nice sandy beach, but few ever want to swim in Lake Superior's cold waters (we did for a minute or two). So other than watching the sun play on the bay, you would probably think that there is nothing more to this village.

There are two things wrong with this. First of all, unless traveling on washboard dirt roads, Grand Marais in not on the way to anywhere. The only good road in or out of Grand Marais is Michigan route 77. It dead ends in town. Grand Marais is in Michigan's upper peninsula, 60 miles northeast of Munising, 25 miles north of Seney (its nearest neighbor) and 45 miles northwest of Newberry. It is nestled along the shores of Lake Superior. Although located at the eastern end of the Pictured Rocks National Lakeshore, it doesn't get near the number of visitors that Munising, on the western edge of the park, does because of its remoteness. The second mistake is that there is a lot more to Grand Marais than the few stores. The trails, dunes, and waterfalls of the National Lakeshore and Grand Marais are definitely worth exploring. More importantly, there are 150 to 300 people (depending on who is doing the telling) who live there year round and their stories are worth listening to.

Like many of Michigan's upper peninsula towns, Grand Marais has had it's ups and downs. It first flourished as a lumber town, and when that business died, the town almost died too. Commercial fishing, some time later, helped to rebuild the town but when that era ended, the town struggled to become known as a tourist spot. It wasn't until the late 70's when the National Park Service took over the care of the *Pictured Rocks* and developed more of the area, that Grand Marais stabilized to what it is today—a retirement and part time tourist community known for its hunting and fishing.

There are six lodging places within walking distance of the town and four more just outside of town. They range from a quaint bed and breakfast in a restored 1887 home on the bay to the new and modern *Welker's Resort* com-plete with restaurant, gift shop, indoor pool and spa. Welker's is not right in town but out at the point; that seemed proper since it was just too modern looking to properly fit into the village itself. The gift shop at Welker's is nothing unusual with its tee shirts and typical tourists do-dads from such places as Taiwan. Except for the Annual Music and Arts festival held the second week in August, the town is not crowded with tourists. We camped at *Woodland Township Park and Campground* just four blocks from downtown.

The campground is on a bluff overlooking Lake Superior and each of it's 100 sites has a good share of trees. For us the best part of camping there was being able to walk or bike to town, the lakeshore

or to the Point and it's museums. We even walked to a church on Sunday (it was across from the campground).

At the corner of Randolph Street and Canal Avenue you will see a very large pickle barrel. It is an unique information center but was not built for that purpose. William Donahey, the author of cartoons and stories about the Teenie Weenies, lived in Grand Marais. In 1926, when he was doing some promotional work for the Murdock Food Co., they suggested that, since the Teenie Weenies lived in a pickle barrel, they would build Mr. Donahey a pickle barrel in which to live. Mr and Mrs. Donahey lived in the pickle barrel on their property during the summers until 1945. After Mr. Donahey died, the barrel was moved to its present location and now serves as the information center.

In Grand Marais, you will not find a touch tone phone, stop light, or mailboxes. Houses do not have street numbers. All mail must be picked up at the post office. I discovered this while in the Pickle Barrel when a gentleman came in and asked the information lady if she knew where his uncle lived. Of course she knew the uncle (everyone knows everyone). The problem was trying to direct him to the house. She mentioned that there are no house numbers or mail boxes and tried to count, in her head, which house was his. She finally said that he should just drive in the right direction then stop at any house. Someone would point out his uncle's house.

One morning be sure to visit *Lefebvre's Fish Market & Bakery*. It is just a block or two east of the post office and a sign points the way. The store is in Shirley Kirkens' house—on her enclosed back porch. Signs out front state that she is famous for her "Sticky Buns" and just above the door a sign says, "get your buns in here." When we walked in, the aroma of freshly baked bread aroused our appetite. There were seven other customers crowded in the small area and Shirley was by the door taking two loaves of bread out of one of the two range type ovens in the front of the store. She apologized for keeping us waiting while she brushed the tops of the loaves with melted butter. She checked the bread in the other oven before resuming her position behind the counter to wait on the next customer. On the counter were two dozen "sticky buns" still hot —having just been released from their pans. They looked like my grandmother's. How could I resist? The display case under the buns was full of donuts and other breads, and to the left, a second display case was full of fresh and smoked fish, turkeys and sausage. We purchased fresh fish, bread and sticky buns. All were so delicious that we couldn't wait to return for more. Those buns were just like my grandmother's.

When I returned another day, Shirley was not busy, so we talked. I was curious as to how and when she started her business and she was eager to share. The "store" opened in 1967 because fishermen in town asked her first husband (Mr. Lefebvre) if he would smoke and sell fish that they caught. Business grew in no time, and Shirley added some baked goods.

Sadly though, on October 31, 1971, her husband and 15 year old son drowned in Lake Superior. Ever hear of the "gales of November" as in the story of the Edmund Fitzgerald? A sudden storm capsized their boat and they were never found. Shirley had to wait seven years to collect the insurance, but she had her business and worked to support her four daughters ages 4, 8, 12 and 14.

She is now remarried and business is better than ever. Vern and Shirley are known for their smoked whitefish, and it was the best we had ever tasted. I asked her if she was afraid of the lake and she admitted that she is. She is glad that her present husband does not like to fish the big lake.

Although there is an IGA grocery store, the *Bayshore Market* and *The General Store*, none sell a big city paper. They sell the local paper which comes out once a week. Asking around, we discovered that the daily paper (the Morning Free Press from Detroit) is sold at the *Superior Hotel* downtown, but the papers don't come in until noon.

When you open the door to the hotel, you will think that you have just entered someone's private home which just happens to have a soda fountain, a candy counter, and two pin ball machines in the living room. The owner, Isabelle (Bess) Capogrosa might be in her kitchen which can be seen from the lobby, but she will quickly greet you. The newspapers are stacked on the counter. She gets about 120 a day. Some she sets aside right away for those who order the paper on a weekly basis, but everyone has to come in and pick up their paper— there are no deliveries. The soda fountain no longer delivers sodas or sundaes, but you can sit on the stool and talk to Bess. We chatted for quite a while. I got a nice history lesson and learned about the local school.

The school is a traditional two story brick building near Lefebvre's on Grand Marais Avenue. Although it says "High School" above the door, we were told that all grades go there from kindergarten to grade 12. There are approximately 80 students in the school, and many grades only have three or four students. Lately the graduation class has numbered around eight, although, Bess told me that she remembered a class of twelve. "But that was the year the twins graduated," she added. The town library is also housed in the school building.

One of the traditions of visiting Michigan's Upper Peninsula is eating a pasty (pass-tee) which is a Cornish meat pie. The oval shaped pasties were brought into the area by the immigrants from Cornwall, England, who came to the peninsula to work in the many iron and copper mines of the 1800's. The pasty was a miner's lunch because it could be carried easily in a pocket and eaten cold or warmed by the lantern's heat. We ate our pasty at the cute *Earl Of Sandwich* shop. It is primarily a deli and ice cream shop with three or four tables, but the pasties were homemade, hot and delicious.

The best place to find out what is going on locally is usually the local bar. *The Dunes Saloon* looked like the place where all the locals go, so we went there too. Shortly after we settled at the bar in hopes of engaging in a little conversation with the bartender, every bar stool (10), and every table and booth (12) were full. Sharon and the cook were the only employees and watching Sharon perform the work of at least three was exhausting. She was smooth, fast, efficient, but we didn't get to talk with her at all. We did overhear the main conversation at the end of the bar and that was mostly anger at the policies of the Department of Natural Resources, especially as they related to fishing. On Friday, we decided to try the Dunes again and this time Pam was the barmaid, waitress, and busperson. She is 35, attractive, wore jeans and a black Harley-Davison tee shirt. Since the place was only one third full, we were able to talk some. Pam moved to Grand Marais six years ago when she became divorced. She is from southern Michigan, but moved to Grand Marais because she thought it would be a good place to raise her children. Her children love it here (there are four in their grade at school), but she is moving them to Marquette (a little over 100 miles west) because she is going to go to college there and was excited about the opportunity. We never did see the cook but can attest to the fact that he/she was busy by the amount of pizzas, hamburgs and nachos that were served both in the saloon and for take out. Do try the pizza. Not only is it the best around, it is the only one.

If you are in Grand Marais in late summer, ask where the blueberries are. You will be directed east five miles then north on a trail type road. If you don't have a truck or four wheel drive, you can walk a mile or so; every bit of effort you exert will be worth the taste of the sweet wild berries.

And don't forget to include the National Park in your visit. Be sure to start at the *National Park Maritime Museum* which is located on Coast Guard Point. Besides learning about shipping on the Great Lakes, you can get a schedule of Park Service Visitor Programs. The Au Sable Light Station began beaming its warning to mariners in 1874 and is well preserved, but it is only accessible by trails. We hiked several trails on our own and joined a ranger on a walk to the light station. On that walk we learned about the old shipwrecks which still litter the beach in this treacherous area of the lake. It was amazing to see full hull skeletons from the 1800's. This graveyard area (the beach as well as the waters) are protected. Grand Marais is definitely worth a weeks visit.

From The November 1990 Issue

RON & BARB QUIT PLAYING
And Go To Work In Arkansas

Barb and Ron Hofmeister are not on vacation here in Hot Springs, Arkansas. They are each giving a minimum of 33 hours per week to the National Park as volunteers.

When they first arrived the end of September, they were quite amazed at this little known park which is located within the city of Hot Springs. In fact, Hot Springs National Park is a large part of the city and the reason that the city grew.

The Hofmeisters arrived late on a Saturday afternoon and found their way to the visitor center which is the recently renovated *Fordyce Bathhouse*. Ranger Paul Sullivan greeted the new volunteers warmly and after a short visit, in which they learned their hours and duties, they left to spend the rest of the weekend getting acquainted with the town and learning about the park. Much of the weekend was spent in studying and they reported to work at 9:00 a.m., Tuesday, October 2.

The first week at work was spent learning. They took a half dozen ranger led walks to the springs, toured all three floors of the bathhouse with tour guides and began getting ready to lead those same tours. They learned about the springs, where the water comes from, where it goes, what it is like, how it has been used for healing and what it is like to take a traditional thermal bath in Hot Springs. They even took a bath at one of the bathhouses to enable them to give first hand information to the visitors.

Much of the time at the Fordyce is spent in behind-the-scene projects. Because of Ron's computer knowledge regarding a software program called Lotus, he has been formatting statistical reports for continued use by management. Barb keeps busy filing slides and reorganizing some of the research files.

Barbs favorite part of the job is leading the *Thermal Feature Tours*.

This tour which lasts about 45 minutes, takes the visitors to the two display springs and along the promenade which is behind bathhouse row. The tour ends at the beautiful cascade, a block from the Fordyce. "Everyone is so amazed that the water in the springs is 143° and 4,000 years old," said Barbara. "It is very exciting to be able to help people understand why this area was and is so special, and to share some of the history—the visitors are very appreciative," she added. Barb also has two other favorite jobs. She spends several hours each day at the information desk, and works as a floating interpreter, answering questions about the bathhouse, its furnishings, bath procedures and so on.

Ron also leads the Thermal Feature Tours, works on the information desk and on weekends completely runs the bookstore and theater area. "Yes, it is different to set the alarm, make lunches and go to work five days a week again, but the rewards are the good feeling of helping the National Park Service and meeting interesting people," said Ron. Ron explained that their "weekend" (days off) is Thursday and Friday and going to work after a few days off is often difficult. "I hate Mondays, even when it is Saturday," he quipped.

The visitor center is very busy at this time of the year with many senior citizens touring the area on their way south for the winter months. Fall is also a popular time because of the fall colors and that brings a large number of tourists from Texas and Louisiana. Things will slow down in November, and Barb and Ron hope to cut back to only three (four at the most) days a week. They want to have time to do some touring and hiking in the area.

Barb and Ron are scheduled to volunteer until the first of December, but will leave a little early to drive their car to Michigan for Susie's wedding on December 1. They will leave the motorhome in the campground under the watchful eye of the National Park Rangers. Barb and Ron said that volunteering was something that they would like to do often. Barbara commented, "It is fun to be a part of a team and community for a while, but I will be ready to move on to new sights in December."

From The September 1991 Issue

FROM YOSEMITE TO OREGON

It was tough to leave Yosemite. We had made so many friends and really loved our work in the History Center. Our last night in Wawona was very special. We attended our last barn dance in the old grey barn, and it was all the more special because Mary and Stacy (those Crane Flat girls) came all the way from their campground to see us. The barn dances were really fun since Ron and I were finally getting the hang of it all, but that night it was mixed with lots of tears and much sadness as the evening came to a close. When the dance was over, we walked through the Pioneer History Center and up our hill one last time. And on Sunday, morning July 28, we pulled out of that special campsite at about 10 a.m. We could see the "pioneers" getting ready to open up as we drove on down the road and I cried again. It had been a wonderful summer full of many great memories.

Our drive was easy—only four hours—and we arrived at a KOA (Kampgrounds Of America) campground in Lodi at about two in the afternoon. We choose this private campground because it was close to the Plymouth dealer where we had an appointment to deliver the car at 8 a.m. Monday.

Once we had the car taken care of, we went to our new home for a week—a CCC in *Isleton*.

We were quite surprised at the area. Lots of waterways; a brochure states that there are over 1,000 miles of waterways in the Sacramento Delta. We choose the area because it was near Robert's apartment and not far from San Francisco and Napa Valley. We were hungry to do some real sightseeing, but were still without wheels so Tuesday morning, we jumped on our bikes and explored 20 miles along the Levee. It was great riding, and we hadn't done such a ride in months. It felt good!! On Wednesday, we got up early, drove the car to Lodi, waited for the fan to be installed, shopped at a farmers market, took the food home, put it away and took off for Napa Valley. It was fantastic to be able to do some touring. Thursday, we stayed close to home, did laundry and relaxed. Robert and Dean came over for dinner and we celebrated Robert's birthday one day early. Friday we took off again for Napa Valley, and this time we knew what we were doing.

NAPA VALLEY, is that area of California which begins at San Pablo Bay, just northeast of San Francisco, and continues north about 30 miles. This narrow valley (from one to five miles wide) is protected by low mountains on the east and west and is kissed by the bay area fog. If you stop in at the visitor center in the town of Napa Valley, south end of the valley, you can pick up a detailed map which outlines the only two north-south routes through the valley and shows each winerie's location. On the back there is a list of each winerie's services, hours,

whether or not they give tours, etc. We were overwhelmed. There are over 200 wineries in the valley. Where does one start? We really arrived too late to do much the first day and the gal at the visitor center suggested we tour one winery which was near by. *Domaine Chandon Winery* is owned by a French company and gave a very informative tour. We learned all about the Pinot Noir grape which grows best in the southern part of the valley. Valley temperatures can vary as much as 10-12 degrees from one end of the valley to the other. We also learned about the fermentation process for the champaign made at that winery. We were all set for a tasting session at the end of the tour and were surprised to find that they do not offer "tastes"—you may buy a glass of champaign and enjoy some free crackers and cheese. We are not fond of sparkling wines anyway, so we said adieu.

Looking at the hours of the other wineries, we realized that the tour had left us with little remaining time. One that was still open was De Moor Winery. There were no tours there, but after buying a souvenir wine glass for $1.50, we could taste the wines they were featuring. We did and liked their Chenin Blanc enough to buy two bottles. We stopped at another winery, but I don't even remember the name. It wasn't very memorable, and we drove the length of the valley just looking out at the neat rows of grape vines on the sides of the hills. The mist was rolling in and it looked as pretty as a soft French painting. When we got to St. Helena at the northern end of the valley, we saw the BIG wineries—Christian Brothers, Beringer, and Krug. Their buildings were elegant and large with paths through lush flower gardens. We knew we had to come back.

On Friday, we arrived in time for the first tour at Christian Brothers Winery. What a class operation. This tour was historical—telling how the religious order used to have a dairy farm but realized there was more money to be made in wine. During prohibition, they had no problem staying in business because they sold wines for communion. The joke was that people turned to religion—at least communion—more during that time. When the tour ended, we found ourselves in an exquisitely furnished lounge and were taught the fine art of wine tasting; it was really quite a lesson. Three wines were tasted, starting with a dry white, then semi-dry red and ending with a dessert wine. From there, we hurried over to the Krug Winery for the 11 am tour; they only have three tours a day. Just across the street, the *Charles Krug Winery* has the distinction of being the oldest winery still in operation. This tour was a little historical but concentrated more on the making of the wine. Again, at the end, we had another lesson (a little different) in wine tasting and were able to sample three different wines.

These tours are great if you have ever been apprehensive about opening wine bottles. They do a good job of showing you how to do it properly and with the least amount of effort. For lunch we went into *St. Helena* and chose to eat at the *Spring Street Restaurant*. It was charming and the pasta salad was delicious. Our last tour of the day was at the *Beringer Winery* and again we were impressed with all we learned and the class of the operation. If you ever get a chance to go to Napa Valley, plan on a whole day at least, and I would suggest starting with the three I just mentioned. If there is time, stop at any of the others.

Saturday morning early, we drove to San Francisco to see Robert and the Coast Guard Cutter Sherman off. It was sad to say goodbye again, and I realized that saying goodbye is a part of our lifestyle. It was interesting to see some of what goes on when a ship leaves port. Ron remarked that he'd like to see what is involved in getting David's ship (the aircraft carrier Eisenhower) underway.

Since we were already in town, we did some shopping in *Mc Donald's Book Store*. They boast being the largest used book dealer in town and I found what I wanted, an out-of-print copy of Lady Bird Johnson's *A White House Diary*. I can now read up on her before we go to the ranch. At the computer store I got the new 5.0 version of Ms Dos and at *Stacy's Book Store*, a big modern bookstore with every kind of book in the world, we bought *Means of Ascent* (LBJ history).

We left Isleton on Sunday and headed north on US 101. Our first stop was near the lumbering town of **Garberville**. Since it was only to be a one night stop, we immediately hopped in the car to do a little touring. The drive on a narrow mountain road west to *Shelter Cove* was a treat. It is right on the ocean. What a place—What a view!! For dinner we ate a yummy hamburg and french fries at *The Blue Moon Saloon* back in Garberville. It was fun to eavesdrop on all the local conversation and we met Von Aie. She told us to be sure and stop in **Phillipsville** on our way out in the morning and eat breakfast at her mom's place (*Road Runner Cafe*). We don't normally stop for breakfast but decided we would this time, and enjoyed a good breakfast and lots of good conversation with her mom and step-father. They dream of full-timing as soon as their youngest graduates. We said we would tell them when the book is ready.

The
Victorian towns
of
Ferndale & Eureka

After breakfast the drive was short and easy. We stayed on US 101 until we saw the sign for Ferndale. Many people told us not to miss this town even though it meant going out of our way (seven miles west of 101). Totally charming and beautifully Victorian is the best way to describe the town. Each and every house is well preserved, brightly painted and adorned with well manicured yards. And the three block downtown area was just as interesting. We parked the motorhome and car in a free lot designed for RVs and walked the streets. The first store we visited supplied us with a map and description of each of the shops. In our travels, we have visited many towns and we look in many stores that seem to have the same merchandise, but these stores and their goods were unique. The *Mercantile* was one of the highlights of the town. It was like going into a museum but everything was really for sale. I have no idea where it came from, but you could buy such things as Fels Naphtha soap, or liniments, old buttons, hardware, shoes (all old fashioned), and candy. Remember those strips of paper that held lots of colored candy dots that we used to buy for a penny? They sold those too but now the price is 30 cents.

Ferndale has become famous in the last 30 years for their annual *Kinetic Sculpture Race* held over the Memorial Day weekend. One enters the race by building some sort of contraption that can be pedaled.

There was a small museum in town where many of the past sculptures are on display. We were amazed at the imagination of some and swore we were in some Disney movie lot. Hobart Brown, local sculptor, started this race when he built a five wheel contraption out of his son's tricycle and a few in town thought they could build something better. The race was on and last year some 54 strange contrivances from six states entered. Brown has a store in town. As soon as we entered the shop, we could tell he was a genius and maybe a bit crazy too. He lives up above the store and invites any who want to see his apartment, to do so. For a one dollar donation you can just walk up stairs and look around. We did, but it sure felt strange to walk through the apartment when no one was there. It looked like something you'd see in a Disney movie— art (junk?) here and there. Interesting!

Eureka is a large city in Northern California right on Hwy 101. Although not nearly as neat and pretty as Ferndale, we did enjoy riding our bikes up and down the streets admiring all the pretty houses. The thing everyone must do while in Eureka is eat at the *Samoa Cook House*. It is the last surviving lumberman's cook house in the west and the food is both plentiful and tasty. When we arrived for lunch, we were seated at a long table. With the clanging of pots and pans, it was noisy but all part of the atmosphere. There's no menu—you get what is being served and it is all family style; the beginning was a tureen of soup, a big bowl of salad and a basket heaped with homemade bread—big thick slices. Lunch was a breaded pork chop, potatoes, gravy, vegetables and dessert.

R E D W O O D NATIONAL PARK weaves in and out of private and state park lands in the northern part of California. The park begins about 16 miles south of Oregon and runs down the coast for about 50 miles. The tall trees are everywhere and we were impressed with the difference between these and their cousin—the Giant Sequoia. They do grow taller but most impressive was the denseness of the forest. We went on an informative ranger walk, spent time in the visitor centers, and took a couple of hikes on our own. One was to see the tallest trees in the world. The hike down was easy—coming up was tough—very steep, but it was well worth it all.

We camped in a CC campground at **Klamath** and did a lot of driving. One very special treat was dining at the *Requa Inn*. It was very elegant, the food was superb, and the owners very friendly. This out-of-the-way place should be a must on everyone's list. After dinner, we took a drive along the rugged coast and watched the fog roll in as the sun set.

OREGON

On Aug 11, we crossed the border into Oregon and love everything we have seen here. The people are friendly and it is fun to shop here because there is no sales tax. We entered the state on Hwy 199 and drove through Cave Junction, they were having some sort of festival and it looked like fun. From there we went through Grants Pass and southeast to Talent, a suburb of Medford, where we had reservations at a CCC.

Ashland just south of Talent is famous for their summer Shakespeare plays. They have three theaters and all summer long run three different Shakespearean plays. One theater is out of doors, and we marveled at the stage. The theaters take turns having a matinee, so they have four performances a day. We inquired about getting tickets but were told they are always sold out for two weeks. From all appearances it looked like a scholarly town with many art and book stores. The shops were very expensive too. Many classical concerts are held during the summer months in the beautiful city park.

Jacksonville, is a lovely historic old mining town full of fun shops and good places to eat just a short distance from Medford. We spent a whole day there. We ate lunch on the patio at *Bella Union* (4*), toured the town on *Sam's Trolley*, browsed the many shops, spent at least one hour in the museum which was in the old court house,

and visited the Beekman house. This house was owned by one of the prominent citizens of the day and is now open as living history. Since we had just spent two months in living history, we thought it would be fun to see how someone else does it. Ron and I both felt that we had truly gone back in time. The maid greeted us and showed us the kitchen and her room. Then we met Mrs Beekman who showed us the parlor and answered our questions about her life. Selznick couldn't have cast a more perfect looking lady to play the part of this elderly woman from 1911. To help us tour the upstairs of the house, we were introduced to her niece. It was wonderful!

CRATER LAKE NATIONAL PARK

is less than 100 miles northeast of Medford, so it was another easy drive. The campground was one of the  nicest national park campgrounds we had ever been in. The spaces were very wide and the trees made a nice privacy fence on three sides. The lake is a wonder. It was a volcano. About 7,000 years ago it erupted with 42 times the force of Mt. St. Helen and the mountain caved in on itself. Over the years, the snow that fell there has melted and filled up the lake. This park gets an average of 50 feet of snow annually and winter is from the end of September to mid June. The lake is the bluest blue I have ever seen. It is the color of a bottle of ink. This very clear lake is 1,932 feet deep at its deepest. We hiked down to the lake edge (one mile—very steep) and took the ranger guided boat trip around the lake. The hike back up was equal to hiking up 150 flights of stairs to the 75th floor of a building. It was not an easy trip but well worth it. We had intended to ride our bikes around the lake (33 miles), but the grades were much too steep for me. It was either going up (6% grades for up to two miles) or going down—there was no level ground. Even with all the hiking, the three days that we spent there were very restful.

La Pine and Bend are just north of Crater Lake on Hwy 97. This central part of Oregon is high desert. Elevation in Bend is about 3,500 feet and it is surrounded by snow capped mountains. *Mt. Bachelor* is world famous for skiing, and we made a little trip there to check out the chair lifts. It was warm (75⁰) when we started up the chair lift, but it was about 50⁰ degrees and windy when we got to the top and yes, there was snow still up there. I just can't get over seeing snow so late in August.

The High Desert Museum should be a must on anyone's list. It is located just a few miles south of town and when you go, allow several hours to see it all. There are many interesting displays on history and geography and every half hour, they have a demonstration of something. We particularly enjoyed a half hour program on birds of prey. This part of Oregon does not get the rain and mist that the coast does but there is no shortage of water here—everyone is watering lawns day and night and the rivers are full and fast. Several National Forests surround the area and there are many things to see and do here. Lakes and rivers are great for fishing, boating and rafting. One can enjoy everything from hiking to antique shopping. We are in Bend as I write this. We'll have the newsletter printed here. I also had a physical here, and we both had our eyes examined and have new glasses. If I had to choose a place to live—right now—I would pick Bend. The people, the town, the facilities, the culture, everything is here. It is a town of about 20,000 people and even though there is a mall and many of the typical stores on the main drag (US 97), there is a downtown and not one store is vacant. And it is not real easy to get downtown because of the one way streets and the fact that it is off the beaten path. There are three square blocks of all kinds of stores that people need. Not tourist stuff but real shops. Downtown is alive and there is ample parking. There is a medical center here with 36 doctors, x-ray, lab, pharmacy and right across the street from the very modern hospital.

So that is what we have been seeing these last few weeks. We plan to get over to Oregon's coast when we leave here on Friday September 6 and from there we will head to Washington. There are so many things to see and places to go.

From the November 1991 issue

UTAH'S FIVE NATIONAL PARKS

ARCHES & CANYONLANDS NATIONAL PARKS, MOAB, UTAH, are about 30 miles apart in the southeast corner of Utah. The Rocky Mountains of northern Utah disappear and are replaced with red Navajo sandstone carved by Mother Nature into mountains of interesting shapes. It is desert country and every bit as beautiful as Sedona, Arizona. But we felt more at home in Moab. Visitors were here to hike, not shop, and the shops sold moderately priced goods. There was one golf course nestled up against the red rocks with fairways and greens fit for a pro tournament and prices for anyone's pocketbook. We split our time in Moab between golf, hiking, and sightseeing.

The very first hike we took was a "moderately strenuous" ranger-led hike into a labyrinth of sandstone fins (narrow walls) called the *Fiery Furnace*. It was a three-hour walk/talk over, under and around two miles of "slickrock" so called be-

cause of ever present lose sand on top. Several passages were so narrow that we had to climb up the sides of the walls a little like spiders (one foot on each side) to get to a wider area. Oh it was great fun, and we wouldn't have been able to do it without the ranger as there are no trails in the furnace. We did think the hike should have been labeled "strenuous."

We hiked just about every "day-hike" in the park (11 total miles) and each took us to new heights and sights. The arches in this park are plentiful and big. One feels so tiny in the presence of them. The other rock formations were also spectacular but too difficult to explain. It was fun to give the shapes our own names—reminiscent of naming clouds.

We didn't know that Moab is the mountain bike capitol of the world until we got there. We wondered why every car and truck was carrying mountain bikes. Near the national park is a national forest site with a slickrock trail just for bikes (and many trails for four wheel drive vehicles). We decided not to try it since we had all we could do to walk on the rocks and we had already biked into the canyon.

We drove into Canyonlands and stopped at all the scenic turnouts. This park is very difficult to see without getting out of the car. The paved roads are few and short, but the sight of the canyon from the different vantage points was special.

Nearby are the La Sal Mountains and a scenic loop road. That drive took us up out of the desert and into the tall pine area. It was a lovely drive with the Aspens in bright yellow dressing.

This area is really prepared for adventure seekers. Rafting companies, jeep and bike rentals are abundant. Brochures on hiking or biking trails, drives, restaurants and so on are available at the Chamber of Commerce office.

We tried out three Moab res- taurants and thoroughly en- joyed the exper- iences. *Dos Amigos Mexican Cantina* served wonderfully spicy, Mexican food. *Eddie McStiff's Brew Pub & Restaurant* was a very relaxing place with a great Chicago style pizza. Everything else that we saw being delivered looked great too.

The *Grand Old Ranch House* on the National Register of Historic Places was superb. The meal we

had there will be remembered for a long time. They boast serving authentic German dishes, prime rib, seafood, steaks and desserts. We opted for the German Sauerbraten. Dinner included delicious home-made soup and salad which was out of this world because of the home-made dressings. Ever hear of champagne walnut or orange marmalade dressing? We had the first and highly recommend it. Fresh warm bread was served with the salad, and dinner included red cabbage and potatoes. It was the best we have ever had. Our complete dinner which included a drink, dessert and tip came to about $35.

We had a wonderful time in Moab and really enjoyed both parks there.

CAPITOL REEF NATIONAL PARK is southwest of Moab and near the village of Torrey, Utah. Its main attraction is petrified sand dunes and the giant sinuous wrinkle in the Earth's crust that stretches for 100 miles across south central Utah. This wrinkle which is called the Waterpocket Fold can be seen from a distance, but as in most parks, the best way to see it is up close. There is one road which runs along the Fold, but after just a few miles we gave up on it. It was of the washboard variety, suitable for jeeps or other such vehicles. We did some hiking in the park and drove the scenic drive which was a passable dirt road. At the end of that drive, we hiked into the Grand Wash to see the waterpockets and the names of the early Mormon pioneers who first entered the area. The names are etched in the walls of the Wash.

A very interesting area of the park is **Fruita**. In the middle of this red sandstone desert is a lush valley—the remnants of the Mormon frontier community settled in the 1880's. Fruit trees are abundant and well cared for by the park service. At harvest time, anyone can "pick your own." Red Delicious apples were there for the picking when we visited, and we climbed the ladders provided to pick plenty. A scale and envelopes are provided. It's all on the honor system.

BRYCE CANYON NATIONAL PARK is southwest of Capitol Reef and much higher in elevation. It is not really a canyon like one carved by water, but it has the appearance of one. Carved by wind and rain, the phantomlike rock spires jut out of the earth creating a maze, like never seen before. Entering the park reminded me of the Grand Canyon because it is heavily forested, unlike the red rock desert we had spent several weeks in. We could have been driving into Yosemite, that is, until you walk over to the overlooks and look down.

We really wanted to get down into this canyon. We thought it would be fun to try horseback over hiking. The four-hour ride guaranteed the most spectacular views, but we weren't sure the weatherman would cooperate. It was raining when we arrived. We figured

we would wake up in the morning and see what the weather was like. When we awoke there was one inch of snow on the ground and much more on the trees. Snow on the red rocks promised to be a pretty sight. We headed for the barn and in no time we were off. As we descended into the canyon, the views were indeed breathtaking. Names like Thor's Hammer, Silent City, Queen's Garden and Fairyland Point are just a few which aptly describe the sandstone sculptures. They were even more fairy-like with the fresh white snow which was the first of the season.

Sadly though, our visit was cut one day short when both our heater and furnace decided to quit working. We got through the night okay headed for Zion which is at a lower elevation, and in the part of the state that is called "Dixie."

ZION NATIONAL PARK is the western most of the parks in Utah. From Bryce, we drove scenic route 89 to Rt 9 knowing that it would take us through Zion for a quick peek on our way to the Coast to Coast campground. As we turned on Rt 9, we saw large warning signs. "Tunnel in park—clearance 11' 4." We were okay with four inches to spare, so we continued on. But when we stopped at the entrance station, we were informed that we were too wide to travel through the tunnel safely. For a $10 fee, they would stop traffic so we could travel through the center of the 1.1 mile tunnel. We had no choice but to go on. To reach our destination any other way would mean traveling over 100 additional miles.

The drive through the park was just as spectacular as Yosemite Valley. Instead of granite, the vividly colored cliffs towering above us were Navajo sandstone. Set aside in 1919, Zion is one of the early national parks. The scale is immense; there are sheer cliffs dropping 3,000 feet, massive buttresses, and deep alcoves. Again, in the midst of such grandeur, I felt very small.

It was Friday when we drove through the park, and we had planned to drive there again from our campground on Saturday. We wanted to spend the day driving and hiking. The weather did not cooperate though, and as of this writing, we have still not had the opportunity to visit Zion properly. We have another week in the area, so weather permitting, we will get back. We won't do the most popular hike though. The Narrows is a 16-mile strenuous trip requiring at least one full day. Much of the trip involves wading through the Virgin River. In some stretches barely 18 inches separate canyon sides that loom 2,000 feet high.

Each of these parks was beautiful. Although each had the same basic characteristic (the red sandstone), they were all different. It is not fair to judge which is best, but we really had the most fun at Arches, and Moab. But then we enjoyed Capitol Reef and John and Vally's campground. Oh, but the horseback ride into Bryce was very special. Zion's beauty was awesome and I cried for the magnificence of it all. I can't decide which was best. You'll have to come and see for yourself.

From The October 1992 Issue

NORTHEAST TRAVELS
History, Harbors, Lobsters & Family

We did it again—traveled too far and too fast. And as usual, this trip left us wanting more. But it was fun!!!

NEW YORK Once we had the last newsletter written, we went to *Hamlin Beach State Park* near Rochester so we could go to a Kinkos (printers) and get it printed. We only stayed three days, and included short visits with two sets of aunts, uncles and cousins.

This was our second visit to western New York and we really wanted to see some areas we had seen before and add new sights, but were limited to choose just one new spot— **Watkins Glen**. Ron had been there a long time ago on a school trip and wanted to share it with me. We stayed at *Sampson State Park* on *Seneca Lake*.

From our base at the campground, we went in several directions. First we visited the Glen and hiked the three-mile-832 stair step trail. It was beautiful. We decided to stay for *Timespell*— a laser light show in the gorge. If you go there, miss this one. It was a big disappointment. One day we took our bikes to nearby **Geneva** and biked a 37-mile route from the book *20 Bicycle tours in the Finger Lakes* by Mark Roth & Sally Walters. The tour took us through rural farmlands and the quiet towns of **Phelps** and **Gorham**. It was an easy ride, but the day was too hot for it to be comfortable. Another day, we drove to **Corning**, home of *Corning Glass Works*, and spent the whole day between *The Corning Museum of Glass*, *The Hall of Science and Industry* and *The Steuben Glass Factory*. We did not do the winery tours (16) since we had just done some in Michigan, and we had to pass up the Mark Twain Musical Drama in Elmira and the Genesee Country Museum. Both were highly recommended. The town of Waterloo looked inviting too. Next time!

Sunday, August 25, we headed east from Seneca Lake on route 20. It was a lovely drive through neat towns with big beautiful houses. **Skaneateles** was especially attractive and we wished we could have stayed a while. As the country got hillier, the motorhome struggled so badly that we had to unhook. I drove the car and led the way to the Coast to Coast Campground at **Gansevoort** which was a little north of **Saratoga Springs**. One of the first things we happened upon, once settled, was a farmer's market. It was very small, near the village green—no more than a dozen vendors; we bought beets, carrots, corn, cucumber, potatoes, radishes, home made apple cinnamon bread and overdosed on veggies the next two days. We visited the *Saratoga National Battlefield* and decided to bike the 10-mile circle route rather than drive. It was a wonderful ride but again very hot, and since we hadn't planned to bike, we were not properly dressed for it. After visiting the park, we discovered the charm of **Saratoga**. It was the racing season, so it was a busy place. No, we did not go to the track, nor did we visit the famous mineral baths, the National Museum of Dance, the Saratoga Harness Hall of Fame, or the National Bottle Museum. We did do a little browsing up and down main street. I never saw so many "horsey" things in my life. You can buy anything with horses pictured on it in this town. We did visit the *Grant Cottage State Historic Site* a little north of town and were very impressed. It is exactly as it was the minute General Grant died at 8:08 a.m. on July 23, 1885. Grant's son stopped the clock and it sets on the mantel as it was that minute. The strange thing about visiting the cottage is that one has to drive through a prison to get to it. Guards order you not to stop until you get to the cottage and give you a big list of do's and don'ts. When a TB sanitarium was built near the cottage, no one ever envisioned that that institution would one day evolve into a prison. It is remarkable that this place has been protected. Credit goes to the dedication of The Friends of Grant Society.

NEW HAMPSHIRE, home of the White Mountains, is a pretty state with a lot of funny names; the Pemigewasset River, Kancamagus Highway and the Wimmipesaukee Railroad were ones we became aware of immediately. We had some bad experiences in New Hampshire so my report may be slanted unfairly against the whole state. Camping in one Coast to Coast Campground was a horrible experience. But that's another story.

Good friends of ours had told us not to miss the "quaint" town of **N. Conway**, so since we were near, we took the drive but got caught in a massive traffic jam. The road into, through and out of N. Conway has large outlet malls—one after another. License plates were from all over, and I am sure there were bar-

gains to be found, but we were not in the mood to fight crowds. We did drive the *Kancamagus Highway* through the *White Mountain National Forest* and found that enjoyable.

MAINE is beautiful in a simple way. The coastal towns, big homes, and seashore are refreshing and the people are very friendly. We arrived in *Acadia National Park* on Sunday, August 30. The weather was perfect, campground rather empty and many ranger activities going on since it was still officially summer. We attended three evening ranger programs in the campground. That is part of what makes camping in a national park so much fun. One day, we got up early, drove to the far side of the park and joined a ranger for a two-hour walk/talk to examine the tide pools. He did a super job of getting the group involved, and everyone learned about the abundance of life in the little puddles of water left behind when the tide goes out. Another day we rode our bikes on many of the carriage roads. In one, less traveled area, we came upon blueberry bushes loaded with ripe berries and picked enough to fill a quart zip-lock bag that we happened to have along. The carriage roads were designed and built by John D. Rockefeller, Jr. in 1915. He saw it as a way to enjoy nature free from the disturbance of the automobile. Doesn't that seem strange since he made his fortune in oil? If we had stayed there three weeks instead of three days, we would still be wanting more, so we are thinking of going back some year as volunteers. Next we visited **Camden**, a delightful seaport village. We stayed at *Robert's Roost Campground* as suggested by good friends and had a nice visit. It is a very picturesque village and we had decided before hand that this seaport village would be where we would try our first lobster. Our campground hostess suggested we try the *Waterfront Restaurant*. It was OK ($15.95 ea.), but now that we have had lobster somewhere else, we know that it was not the best.

We had called the CCC park in *Lebanon, Maine* ahead of time just in case they would let us in over the Labor Day weekend and they said "sure." Most CCC parks only let their own members in on holidays. We had the best time there. The campers and staff were super friendly. Right away we were invited to the breakfasts each morning, the $6 lobster/steak dinner and the Saturday night dance with a live band. For the dinner, Ron had lobster (I had steak) and he raved about it. We did one of our seminars there and it was the best one yet—13 couples attended and they were very interested in full-timing. It was a nice relaxing weekend. We never left the park.

MASSACHUSETTS looks like England—if you are looking at the names of towns on the map. Cambridge, Framingham, Needham, Weymouth, Chelmsford, Leicester, Ipswich and many more are very familiar to us from our travels in England. After having so much difficulty trying to follow route 1A, Ron was fit to be tied, and said that we were not going to tour Boston. This was one of those times when the Interstate would have been better. When we approached the tunnel into Boston, we were told that we couldn't go through. They don't allow RVs because of the propane. In the jumble of traffic, we were hastily told which direction to go, and we promptly got lost for a while.

Once settled in the overgrown and nearly deserted *Wompatuck State Park* southeast of Boston and near the bay, Ron calmed down, and we took off in the car to find the Adams National Historic Site in Quincy. We could not follow the route (no route or street signs) so we gave up. The next day when we got our mail in **Cohasset**, I inquired about the best way to get to Boston. To our delight, we found there is a commuter ferry which leaves every 20 minutes or so, each morning, from nearby *Hingham Harbor*. After checking it out, we decided to go the next morning.

The four dollar, 35 minute trip aboard a large passenger ferry was comfortable, and we were deposited right near the heart of the city.

We easily found the beginning of *The Freedom Trail*, did the first part on our own, then took the free ranger walk/talk for the remainder of the trail. It was a great history lesson.

After we returned to Hingham, we looked for a place to eat and choose *Ye Old Mill Grill*. Their special was stuffed Lobster (stuffed with shrimp & scallops in a cracker base). Dinner included fresh rolls, chowder, french fries, wine and dessert for $13.95. Since Ron had raved about his last lobster, I decided to try again. We both ordered the special, and it was so yummy that I will never, ever forget it. It was something to die for. I hope you can find this place some day. And do go on a Wednesday when they have this special.

When we left the state park, we took the interstate all the way to **Sturbridge** and a CCC park only a few miles from *Old Sturbridge Village*. It was billed as living history, and they did a pretty good job. I was expecting that every one would be in 1833, but some do and some don't. I understand that weekends are not the best time to visit if you want real first person living history. We went on a weekend. The admission price allows one to go two days in a row which we did. It was well worth visiting.

NEW YORK (AGAIN). We reentered the state on I-84 and planned to stay at a campground in **Fishkill**. It was so run down that we got out the ole *Trailer Life Campground Directory* and found a nice KOA in **Plattekill**. It was expensive, but a perfect location for our planned visit with Ron's daughter Susie, her husband Ross and one year old daughter Taylor. Since they live so near **West Point** we included a guided tour there which we highly recommend. From the visitor center just outside the Thayer Gate, one can choose either the short (1 hr) or long (1 hr 45 min) bus tour. We choose the longer one because it included the cemetery and more history. The price was reasonable ($5.50 ea.) and our tour guide was great.

Our campground was near **Hyde Park** and two other special places—*Roosevelt and Vanderbilt National Historic Sites*. We went one day, and visited both homes with Susie and little Taylor, learning just enough to make us want to delve into the histories. Ron and I went back another day and got completely lost in all the documents and history in the *FDR Library and Museum*. We were also able to include a tour of Eleanor Roosevelt's cottage nearby.

The Frederick & Louise Vanderbilt home was garishly typical of those of the Gilded Age. They had no children, so after Frederick's death in 1938, Margaret Van Alen (Louise's niece) inherited the estate and all it's furnishings. She already had several mansions of her own and couldn't afford to take care of it. When she heard of the neighbor's (FDR) plan to donate his home to the park service, she did the same—for a nice tax write-off. It has been a ward of the National Park Service since 1940.

FDR's home was the exact opposite—very simple and homey. I did not know that FDR was an only child, that his home belonged to his domineering mother and that Eleanor raised her five children there with her mother-in-law, who really ran the show. Lots of neat history prompted me to buy two very large books. All this touring just whets my appetite for more information.

NEW JERSEY is where Ron's sister Linda and her family live. That was the reason for our visit there. We found a nice State Park (*Cheesequake*) near their home in East Brunswick and enjoyed three days of catching up on family. It was here that we got word that Ron's mom needed more help than she thought she would after her bunion surgery. We were planning to be in Florida by mid November, but offered to go early if she needed us. She did. But first we had to see Ron's son David, before he took off for his three-year stint in Spain.

To get to *Norfolk*, we decided to take the ferry from *Cape May*. It was a short drive from Cheese-quake. After we got settled in the Coast to Coast Campground, we spent the afternoon touring that Victorian town, then went to bed early so we could get up early and meet the ferry. It was a wonderful way to get through the congested areas along the coast. We stayed in the motorhome during the whole 70-minute trip. Ron sat in his chair reading the paper and drinking coffee while I worked on the computer. What a way to travel!!

VIRGINIA. Our four-day visit in **Norfolk** was all visit. It was a talking, game playing, meals-together kind of visit, with Dave and Evelyn. We had planned to do some camping with them (they are real campers—tent style), but tropical storm Danielle hung close to shore, kept us soggy and forced us to change our plans. We really felt bad, because they had their gear all set to go.

So here we are in **Florida**. We drove two straight days to get here. We have settled into a very nice private campground in **Winter Haven**. Joe and Jenny Hofmeister (no relation) are the owners of the *Holiday Trav-l-Park* here and gave us a nice spot for the month. For the off season monthly rate of $245, we can spend lots of time helping Ron's mom (Ron is doing it all now while I crank this out) and we will have plenty of time to get some other stuff done. The awning is not working correctly on one side, we have a leak some-where in the cabover section (around a window I think), the bikes need cleaning and oiling (the chains are orange from so much rain), both vehicles need oil changes, I need a permanent and so on. Next month I'll let you know how the handyman did.

♥ ⌂ ♥

APPENDIX B

HELPFUL ADDRESSES

INSURANCE

Insurance Companies that have
experience insuring full-timers.

Alexander & Alexander
700 Fisher Building
Detroit, MI 48202-3053
Toll Free 1-800-521-2942

National General Insurance Company
Good Sam Vehicle Insurance Plan
P.O.Box 66937
St. Louis, MO 63166-9908
Toll Free 1-800-847-2887 ex 5765

National General Insurance Company
Protection Coast to Coast Insurance Plan
(same address as above)

RV ROAD SERVICE

Good Sam Emergency Road Service
P. O. Box 10205
Des Moines, IA 50380-0205
Toll Free 1-800-234-3450

Coast to Coast Emergency Road Service
64 Inverness Drive, E.
Englewood, CO 80112
Toll Free 1-800-368-5721

Foremost TravelSure RV Insurance Program
Deptartment 214, P.O. Box 3357
Grand Rapids, MI 49501
Toll Free 1-800-262-0170, ext 214

Road America RV Assist
225 Alcazar Avenue
Coral Gables, FL 33134-9672
Toll Free 1-800-443-4187

FOR MEMBERSHIP INFORMATION:

Family Motor Coach Association
8291 Clough Pike
Cincinnati, OH 45244-9976
Toll Free 1-800-543-3622

Escapees
100 Rainbow Drive
Livingston, TX 77351
Toll Free 1-800-9Rovers (976-8377)

The Good Sam Club
P.O. Box 6885
Englewood, CO 80155-9896

Coast to Coast Campgrounds
64 Inverness Drive E.
Englewood, CO 80112
Toll Free 1-800-368-5721

RVing Women
201 E Southern Ave
Apache Junction, AZ 85219
ph: 602-983-4687

Loners on Wheels
PO Box 1355
Poplar Bluff, MO 63901

Loners of America
Rt 2 Box 85E
Ellsinore, MO 63937-9520

SMART Inc. (Special Military Active
Retired Club)
600 University Blvd. Suite 1A
Pensacola, FL 32504

Christian Camper Club
PO Box 606
Homeland, CA 92348
ph: 818-343-3881

**RV MAGAZINES AND
CAMPGROUND DIRECTORIES**

Trailer Life
P O Box 55793
Boulder,CO 80322-5793

Motorhome
P.O. Box 54461
Boulder, CO 80322-4461

KOA Directory, Road Atlas
& Camping Guide
send $3.00 to: KOA Directory
Dept. FMC, P.O.Box 30162
Billings, MT 59107

Trailer Life Campground & RV
Services Directory
P.O. Box 6060
Camarillo, CA 93011

Woodall's Campground Directory
Dept 1693 (F)
28167 North Keith Drive
Lake Forest, IL 60045-5000
Toll Free 1-800-323-9076

Workamper News
201 Hiram Road
Heber Springs, AR 72543
Toll Free 1-800-446-5627

OTHER USEFUL ADDRESSES:

Golf Card information

Golf Card International Corp.
P.O. Box 7022
Englewood, CO 80155
Toll Free 1-800-453-4260

Voice mail service

Voice Tel of Colorado
1660 S Albion Street Suite 606
Denver, CO 80222-4022

Medical Emergency Service   Service includes
air ambulance and RV return.

Travel Assistance International
Dept. FMCA, 1133 15th St., N.W., Suite 400
Washington, D.C. 20005
Toll Free 1-800-821-2828

Medical Air Service Association (MASA)
9 Village Circle Suite 540
Roanoke, TX 76262
Toll Free 1-800-423-3226

Books

RV Owners Handbook (Vols 1,2 & 3)
100 Corporate N
Suite 100
Bannockburn, IL 60015

Survival of the Snowbirds
Rovers Publishing
100 Rainbow Drive
Livingston, TX 77351-9300

Guide to Free Campgrounds
Cottage Publications
24396 Pleasant View Drive
Elkhart, IN 46517

♥ ⌂ ♥

GLOSSARY

ATMs: Automated Teller Machines.

Automatic levelers: Built in hydraulic jacks that operate from the motorhome console.

Black water: Sewage from toilet held in its own holding tank.

Boondocking: Camping free without hook-ups.

Cabover: Top front section of camper body that extends forward over the cab of the truck.

Cash flow projections: Estimating income and expense for a specific period showing beginning and ending balance.

Class A motorhome: A motorhome with the living unit constructed on a bare, specially designed chassis.

Class C motorhome: A conventional motorhome built using a manufacturer's chassis and cab. The bed portion extends over the cab.

Dry camping: Camping without hook-ups.

Dump station: Station where waste tanks are dumped into a sewage system.

Fifth-Wheel travel trailer: A travel trailer built with a raised forward section that allows a bi-level floor plan. It is usually pulled by a pickup truck with a specially designed hitch which is installed in the bed of the truck.

Grey water: Used water from shower and sink.

Gross Axle Weight (GAW): Total weight a given axle, suspension and tires are designed to carry.

Gross Combination Weight Rating (GCWR): Total loaded weight of trailer and tow vehicle combination as established by the vehicle manufacturer. Includes vehicle and trailer weight, equipment, gas water, passengers and payload.

Gross Vehicle Weight: Actual weight of fully equiped and loaded vehicle including passengers, gas, and payload. Must not exceed the Gross Vehicle Weight Rating.

Gross Vehicle Weight Rating (GVWR): Total loaded weight of a vehicle as established by the manufacturer. Includes vehicle weight, equipment, gas, water, passengers and payload. This must not be exceeded.

Holding tanks: Tanks built into the RV to hold wastes from sink, shower, toilet etc.

Hookups: Refers to one or all of the following: water, sewer, electricity, cable.

Inverter: Changes battery current (direct) to alternating current.

Phone dialer: Device that fits over the mouthpiece of a telephone and when activated emits tones consistent with a push button phone.

Pickup Camper: Camper body that fits into the bed of a pckup truck.

Pull-throughs: Campsite designed to allow a towing vehicle to enter and exit without backing up.

Roof storage pod: A large fiberglass storage container anchored on the roof of the RV.

Setup: Those activities necessary to hook-up and level the RV into a camp site.

Slide out: That portion of the RV that extends from the main body to enlarge the RV. Usually found on fifth-wheels and a few motorhomes and travel trailers.

Tow Dolly: Two wheeled trailer that is designed for placing the front wheels of the towed vehicle on the trailer.

Towed vehicle: Vehicle being towed.

Towing vehicle: Vehicle towing fifth-wheel or travel trailer.

Travel Trailer: Non powered RV unit with rigid walls and roof, designed to be towed.

VIP: Volunteer In Parks, as referred to by the National Park Service

♥ ⌂ ♥

INDEX

—*Sayles Studio, Kingwood, Texas*

ABOUT THE AUTHORS

RON HOFMEISTER retired in March of 1989 after a distinguished career with the Michigan Department of Transportation. He retired as Deputy Director for Finance, overseeing all financial operations and a budget of 1.1 billion dollars. Prior to his appointment as Deputy Director, he was in charge of the department's financial operations for fifteen years and budget controller of the Maintenance Division for seven years. In his managerial positions, Ron had many opportunities to listen to and council employees as to their career ambitions and goals. However, he found that many of them were surprisingly vague and unsure of their retirement years. It was not unusual to observe a retired employee wistfully visiting the former work site appearing lost. Hence, this book about an exciting and affordable lifestyle, that is tailor-made for the retiree.

With his financial background, it is not surprising that Ron pays particular attention to the economic aspect of the full-timing lifestyle.

BARBARA HOFMEISTER was a sales trainer, motivational speaker and a top Tupperware manager before she and Ron adopted the nomadic life of being full-timers. Her ability to manage, direct and organize is especially evident in her chapter on "Getting Ready". Her success in meeting and drawing out people along the way is also apparent in the newsletter (Movin' On) that she writes. Whether it's a new location or meeting new people, she is anxious to learn. Her greatest asset being that she loves to ask questions and she *listens*.

WANT MORE COPIES TO GIVE AS GIFTS?
Fill out the order form below and mail it to us:

Ron and Barb Hofmeister
101 Rainbow Drive #2179
Livingston, Texas 77351-9300

Order Form

Please send _____ copies of

An Alternative Lifestyle—Living & Traveling
Full-Time in a Recreational Vehicle
At $12.95 per Copy
(Plus Shipping & Tax if applicable) To
PLEASE PRINT OR TYPE)

NAME_____

ADDRESS_____

_____

Total Amount_____

Shipping (Priority Mail)
& Handling $4.00 ea)_____

Texas Residents add
7.25% Sales Tax
(.94 per book)_____

Amount Enclosed_____

Please make checks payable to R & B Publications
and allow 2-4 weeks for delivery. Thank You

WOULD YOU LIKE TO SUBSCRIBE
TO *MOVIN' ON* ?

Movin' On is not a money making venture, but we would be glad to include you on our list if you like. We try to put out at least six issues per year, and usually get out as many as ten. It depends on where we are—sometimes we are in remote areas and can't get to a printer. Each issue costs us $1.50 to print and mail. Our friends give us $9.00 to cover approximately one years worth. We keep track on the mailing label so you'd know how many more issues you have paid for. For example, the first label would say 5 (meaning you will get five **more** issues) and the next would say 4, then 3, 2, 1 and 0. When you get to zero, you know you should send us a check if you want to be kept on the mailing list.

If interested please fill out the order form below and mail it to us:

Ron and Barb Hofmeister
101 Rainbow Drive #2179
Livingston, Texas 77351-9300

ORDER FORM

Please send me _____ issues of *Movin' On* at $1.50 per issue to (PLEASE PRINT OR TYPE)

NAME_____

ADDRESS_____

CITY_____STATE_____ZIP_____

AMOUNT ENCLOSED_____FOR_____ISSUES.

Please make check or money order out to R & B Publications and send to the above address.

Notes

Notes

Notes